THE PELICAN SHAKESPEARE
GENERAL EDITOR : ALFRED HARBAGE
AB30
ALL'S WELL THAT ENDS WELL

WILLIAM SHAKESPEARE

All's Well
That Ends Well

EDITED BY JONAS A. BARISH

PENGUIN BOOKS

BALTIMORE · MARYLAND

This edition first published 1964
Penguin Books Inc.
3300 Clipper Mill Road, Baltimore, Maryland 21211

© Copyright 1964
by Penguin Books Inc.

Library of Congress Catalog Card
Number 64-23534

Printed in the United States of America

CONTENTS

CONTENTS

SHAKESPEARE AND HIS STAGE

William Shakespeare was christened in Holy Trinity Church, Stratford-on-Avon, April 26, 1564. His birth is traditionally assigned to April 23rd. He was the eldest of four boys and two girls who survived infancy in the family of John Shakespeare, glover and trader of Henley Street, and his wife Mary Arden, daughter of a small landowner of Wilmcote. In 1568 John was elected Bailiff (equivalent to Mayor) of Stratford, having already filled the minor municipal offices. The town maintained for the sons of the burgesses a free school, taught by a university graduate and offering preparation in Latin sufficient for university entrance; its early registers are lost, but there can be little doubt that Shakespeare received the formal part of his education in this school.

On November 27, 1582, a license was issued for the marriage of William Shakespeare (aged eighteen) and Ann Hathaway (aged twenty-six), and on May 26, 1583, their child Susanna was christened in Holy Trinity Church. The inference that the marriage was forced upon the youth is natural but not inevitable; betrothal was legally binding at the time, and was sometimes regarded as conferring conjugal rights. Two additional children of the marriage, the twins Hamnet and Judith, were christened on February 2, 1585. Meanwhile the prosperity of the elder Shakespeares had declined, and William was impelled to seek a career outside Stratford.

The tradition that he spent some time as a country teacher is old but unverifiable. Because of the absence of records his early twenties are called the "lost years," and only one thing about them is certain — that at least some of these years were spent in winning a place in the acting profession. He may have begun as a provincial trouper, but by 1592 he was established in London and prominent enough to be attacked. In a pamphlet of that year, *Groatsworth of Wit,* the ailing Robert Greene complained of the neglect which university writers like himself had suffered from actors, one of whom was daring to set up as a playwright:

> ... an upstart crow beautified with our feathers, that with his *Tiger's heart wrapt in a player's hide* supposes he is as well able to bombast out a blank verse as the best of you, and being an absolute Johannes-factotum, is in his own conceit the only Shake-scene in a country.

The pun on his name, and the parody of his line "O tiger's heart wrapt in a woman's hide" (*III Henry VI*), pointed clearly to Shakespeare. Some of his admirers protested, and Henry Chettle, the editor of Greene's pamphlet, saw fit to apologize:

> I am as sorry as if the original fault had been my fault, because myself have seen his demeanor no less civil than he excellent in the quality he professes. Besides divers of worship have reported his uprightness of dealing, which argues his honesty, and his facetious grace in writing that approves his art. (Prefatory epistle, *Kind Heart's Dream*)

The plague closed the London theatres for many months in 1593–94, denying the actors their livelihood. To this period belong Shakespeare's two narrative poems, *Venus and Adonis* and *Rape of Lucrece,* both dedicated to the Earl

8

of Southampton. No doubt the poet was rewarded with a gift of money as usual in such cases, but he did no further dedicating and we have no reliable information on whether Southampton, or anyone else, became his regular patron. His sonnets, first mentioned in 1598 and published without his consent in 1609, are intimate without being explicitly autobiographical. They seem to commemorate the poet's friendship with an idealized youth, rivalry with a more favored poet, and love affair with a dark mistress; and his bitterness when the mistress betrays him in conjunction with the friend; but it is difficult to decide precisely what the "story" is, impossible to decide whether it is fictional or true. The real distinction of the sonnets, at least of those not purely conventional, rests in the universality of the thoughts and moods they express, and in their poignancy and beauty.

In 1594 was formed the theatrical company known until 1603 as the Lord Chamberlain's Men, thereafter as the King's Men. Its original membership included, besides Shakespeare, the beloved clown Will Kempe and the famous actor Richard Burbage. The company acted in various London theatres and even toured the provinces, but it is chiefly associated in our minds with the Globe Theatre built on the south bank of the Thames in 1599. Shakespeare was an actor and joint owner of this company (and its Globe) through the remainder of his creative years. His plays, written at the average rate of two a year, together with Burbage's acting won it its place of leadership among the London companies.

Individual plays began to appear in print, in editions both honest and piratical, and the publishers became increasingly aware of the value of Shakespeare's name on the title pages. As early as 1598 he was hailed as the leading English dramatist in the *Palladis Tamia* of Francis Meres:

As Plautus and Seneca are accounted the best for Comedy and Tragedy among the Latins, so Shakespeare among the English is the most excellent in both kinds for the stage: for Comedy, witness his *Gentlemen of Verona,* his *Errors,* his *Love labors lost,* his *Love labors won [Taming of the Shrew?],* his *Midsummers night dream,* & his *Merchant of Venice;* for Tragedy, his *Richard the 2, Richard the 3, Henry the 4, King John, Titus Andronicus,* and his *Romeo and Juliet.*

The note is valuable, both in indicating Shakespeare's prestige and in helping us to establish a chronology. In the second half of his writing career, history plays gave place to the great tragedies; and farces and light comedies gave place to the problem plays and symbolic romances. In 1623, seven years after his death, his former fellow actors, John Hemming and Henry Condell, cooperated with a group of London printers in bringing out his plays in collected form. The volume is generally known as the First Folio.

Shakespeare had never severed his relations with Stratford. His wife and children may sometimes have shared his London lodgings, but their home was Stratford. His son Hamnet was buried there in 1596, and his daughters Susanna and Judith were married there in 1607 and 1616 respectively. (His father, for whom he had secured a coat of arms and thus the privilege of writing himself gentleman, died in 1601, his mother in 1608.) His considerable earnings in London, as actor-sharer, part owner of the Globe, and playwright, were invested chiefly in Stratford property. In 1597 he purchased for £60 New Place, one of the two most imposing residences in the town. A number of other business transactions, as well as minor episodes in his career, have left documentary records. By 1611 he was in a position to retire, and he seems gradually to have withdrawn from theatrical activity in order to live in Stratford. In March, 1616, he made a will, leaving token bequests to Burbage, Hemming, and Condell, but the bulk of his estate to his family. The most famous feature of the will, the bequest of the second-best bed to his wife, reveals nothing about Shakespeare's marriage; the quaintness of the provision seems commonplace to those familiar with ancient testaments. Shakespeare died April 23, 1616, and was buried in the Stratford church where he had been christened. Within seven years a monument was erected to his memory on the north wall of the chancel. Its portrait bust and the Droeshout engraving on the title page of the First Folio provide the only likenesses with an established claim to authenticity. The best verbal vignette was written by his rival Ben Jonson, the more impressive for being imbedded in a context mainly critical:

> ... I loved the man, and do honor his memory (on this side idolatry) as much as any. He was indeed honest, and of an open and free nature: he had an excellent fancy, brave notions, and gentle expressions. ... (*Timber or Discoveries*, c. 1623–30)

The reader of Shakespeare's plays is aided by a general knowledge of the way in which they were staged. The King's Men acquired a roofed and artificially lighted theatre only toward the close of Shakespeare's career, and then only for winter use. Nearly all his plays were designed for performance in such structures as the Globe — a three-tiered amphitheatre with a large rectangular platform extending to the center of its yard. The plays were staged by daylight, by large casts brilliantly costumed, but with only a minimum of properties, without scenery, and quite possibly without intermissions. There was a rear stage balcony for action "above," and a curtained rear recess for "discoveries" and other special effects, but by far the major portion of any play was enacted upon the projecting platform, with episode following episode in swift succession, and with shifts of time and place signaled the audience only by the momentary clearing of the stage between the episodes. Information about the identity of the characters and, when necessary, about the time and place of the action was incorporated in the dialogue. No additional indications of place have been inserted in the present editions; these are apt to obscure the original fluidity of structure, with the emphasis upon action and speech rather than scenic background. The acting, including that of the youthful apprentices to the profession who performed the parts of women, was highly skillful, with a premium placed upon grace of gesture and beauty of diction. The audiences, a cross section of the general public, commonly numbered a thousand, sometimes more than two thousand. Judged by the type of plays they applauded, these audiences were not only large but also perceptive.

THE TEXTS OF THE PLAYS

About half of Shakespeare's plays appeared in print for the first time in the folio volume of 1623. The others had been published individually, usually in quarto volumes, during his lifetime or in the six years following his death. The copy used by the printers of the quartos varied greatly in merit, sometimes representing Shakespeare's true text, sometimes only a debased version of that text. The copy used by the printers of the folio also varied in merit, but was chosen with care. Since it consisted of the best available manuscripts, or the more acceptable quartos (although frequently in editions other than the first), or of quartos corrected by reference to manuscripts, we have good or reasonably good texts of most of the thirty-seven plays.

In the present series, the plays have been newly edited from quarto or folio texts depending, when a choice offered, upon which is now regarded by bibliographical specialists as the more authoritative. The ideal has been to reproduce the chosen texts with as few alterations as possible, beyond occasional relineation, expansion of abbreviations, and modernization of punctuation and spelling. Emendation is held to a minimum, and such material as has been added, in the way of stage directions and lines supplied by an alternative text, has been enclosed in square brackets.

None of the plays printed in Shakespeare's lifetime were divided into acts and scenes, and the inference is that the author's own manuscripts were not so divided. In the folio collection, some of the plays remained undivided, some were divided into acts, and some were divided into acts and scenes. During the eighteenth century all of the plays were divided into acts and scenes, and in the Cambridge edition of the mid-nineteenth century, from which the influential Globe text derived, this divison was more or less regularized and the lines were numbered. Many useful works of reference employ the act-scene-line apparatus established by the Globe text.

Since the act-scene division thus established is obviously convenient, but is of very dubious authority so far as Shakespeare's own structural principles are concerned, or the original manner of staging his plays, a problem is presented to modern editors. In the present series the act-scene division of the Globe text is retained marginally, and may be viewed as a reference aid like the line numbering. A printer's ornament marks the points of division when these points have been determined by a cleared stage indicating a shift of time and place in the action of the play, or when no harm results from the editorial assumption that there is such a shift. However, at those points where the established division is clearly misleading – that is, where continuous action has been split up into separate "scenes" – the ornament is omitted and the distortion corrected. This mechanical expedient seemed the best means of combining utility and accuracy.

The General Editor.

INTRODUCTION

All's Well That Ends Well has always been a stepchild among Shakespeare's plays. Eminent readers have sometimes responded warmly to the figure of Helena, but they have rarely spoken well of the play as a whole. Usually it has been viewed as self-evidently one of Shakespeare's worst, a thing of shreds and patches "scratched over by a master's hand upon a poor original," a repository of juvenile and even fatuous couplets alternating with passages of maturely wrought blank verse, a play in which the conduct of the narrative is undignified, the ethics of the plot, especially the bed trick, reprehensible, the clowning, such as it is, "uncouth," the part of Parolles irrelevant, Bertram irredeemably disagreeable, Helena – for all her virtue – too scheming, and the whole, despite incidental felicities, "a rather nasty play."

It is perhaps useless to answer such criticism by pointing out that it is proceeding largely by negatives, complaining of absences instead of responding to presences. Audiences who insist on ingratiating characters with whom to identify will always find Bertram repellent. Those who stipulate jocosity and high spirits in comic drama will always find the play "mirthless" and "unsmiling." Unquestionably it lacks the festival element of much other Shakespearean comedy: we hear no merry catches, no hunting songs, no amorous strains picked out on lutes; nor do we assist at dances, masques, or revels, at midnight frolics in the buttery, or sportive jesting among young wooers. This lack might prompt us to conclude that Shakespeare's interest was elsewhere, that the creation of a festival mood was remote from his intentions. Of wooing, again, we see but little, and that little of a perverse sort: a young woman in quest of a man who scorns her when she offers herself to him as a bride and then abandons her when she has become his wife. Even the clown of the play is "a shrewd knave and an unhappy," skilled at deciphering the foolishness of the world but undelighted by its delights. And in the denouement, where Shakespeare normally would be working reconciliations and composing harmonies, he creates discords and leaves us doubting and uneasy. But the unconventionality of the wooing, the bleakness of the clown's humor, the ambiguous tone of the close, might in their turn be regarded as positive achievements, as contributing in their various ways to the play's own atmosphere, its special poignance and austere beauty.

All's Well That Ends Well was first printed in the folio of 1623. No external clues exist as to the date of writing or of first performance. Largely on stylistic grounds, and by virtue of resemblances to *Measure for Measure*, it is thought to have been written about the same time as that play (c. 1602–1604), and its links with it, and with *Troilus and Cressida*, have led to its being classified with them as a "problem play" or "problem comedy." By this the critics have sometimes meant that Shakespeare, in the plays in question, was investigating certain ethical issues, or "problems," and at other times that these plays share certain puzzling traits — a crabbedness of language, a preoccupation with disease and sexuality, an alleged "loathing" of spirit, a refusal to fit comfortably into the usual generic categories — that make them "problems" for critics.

Recent comment, more helpfully, has stressed the affinities of *All's Well* with the last plays, and seen it as belonging to the mainstream of Shakespearean comedy. Its "problematic" character would seem best described not by reference to some special state of revulsion, or disillusion, in Shakespeare at the time of writing, but, more prosaically, as a defect of artistic management, a relatively imperfect fusion of elements with which Shakespeare worked throughout his career. Like other Shakespearean comedy, *All's Well That Ends Well* moves between the two poles of romance and satire – between a vision of life as good and gracious, expressed in beneficent magic and marvellous coincidences, and a vision of it as absurd and degraded, expressed in scenes of folly and derision – and with these two modes of vision it merges a third, inherited from the English morality play, of life as a pilgrimage, a quest for salvation, in which men take wrong paths, stray into forests or labyrinths, but ultimately regain the road that leads to fulfillment.

The plot comes from a tale of Boccaccio, translated into English in Painter's *Palace of Pleasure,* one of the most familiar of sixteenth-century collections of Italian stories. Shakespeare reshapes the original narrative freely, but he is careful to preserve, and even insist on, the romance motif, the details suggestive of folklore such as Helena's magic cure of the king, her pilgrimage and mock death, and the lucky coincidences on which the successful working out of events depends.

At the same time he overlays the romance pattern with the morality pattern, making Bertram the central personage in the latter. Older morality drama had presented the hero's life, from birth to death, in a sequence of moral crises understood to be universal and exemplary. One common variant consisted in treating only a single phase of this life-history, usually the moment of young manhood, when the hero, setting forth into the world, fell into temptations peculiar to the young, and at length, after much suffering and wrongdoing, was reclaimed to happiness and virtue. This partial pattern, often consciously derived from the parable of the prodigal son, underlies the career of Bertram. Bertram is the raw youth whose impetuousness leads him swiftly, if not inevitably, into error when he enters the world. He places himself under the tutelage of a braggart, spurns wholesome advice, and behaves dishonorably toward those who love him. In rejecting Helena, he rejects a whole complex of traditional values embodied in the elders of his society — his dead father, his mother, and his king.

His rebellion, however, contains at least one positive element, his eagerness to win fame in battle. Soldiership is one traditional value he does honor, and it becomes the basis for his recovery of the rest. Italy, where he seeks his fortune in war, serves Bertram as the other country and place of exile in which Shakespearean characters often work out their destinies before returning, seasoned and in some measure purified, to resume their rightful posts at home. In Florence Bertram lays claim through his valor to some of the manhood impugned by his earlier acts. He wins the esteem of his seniors and differentiates himself from his cowardly hanger-on Parolles. His earlier acts, meantime, are breeding consequences that affect him in other ways. When he learns, in a rebuking letter from his mother, of the disappearance of Helena, his conscience awakens. He changes, we are told, "almost into another man." The two lords to whom Shakespeare entrusts this report go on to expound, in Shakespeare's gravest aphoristic prose, the ethical drift of the play: "The web of our life is of a mingled yarn, good and ill together; our virtues would be proud if our faults whipped them not, and our crimes would despair if they were not cherished by our virtues." Bertram, viewed in this light, symbolizes errant humanity; the texture of human life, radically multifold, intrinsically compounded of good and ill, makes it certain he will transgress, and the comments of the two lords seem partly designed to mitigate, on this score, the severity of the judgment we might otherwise be tempted to pass, by forcing us to recognize ourselves in Bertram.

While the two lords are discussing him, Bertram is keeping his assignation with Helena, whom he believes to be Diana. Shortly after, he participates in the unmasking of Parolles. The effect of these events is to transfer him decisively from the guardianship of his evil genius Parolles to that of his good genius Helena. But whereas the false glamour of Parolles, a thing of glitter and surface, can be dispelled in a moment, the true worth of Helena is more reticent; it must work slowly and in the dark, its full impact deferred until the final moments of the play.

One aspect of Bertram's story is that it is worked out in terms of a distinction between inherited and achieved nobility. When the play opens, the Countess voices the hope that Bertram will be his father's heir in the true sense, by behaving nobly, by making his father's virtue his own in act. Her implied doubt on this point is confirmed by Bertram's rejection of Helena, where his snobbish insistence on her low origins constitutes in itself a repudiation of his own nobility, of the kind of nobility bequeathed him by a father who conducted himself with particular graciousness toward those of humbler rank. At this moment Bertram misconceives his aristocratic heritage as a simple possession, rather than as a quality of mind or a mode of being. He thinks of it as something totally *his*, to be guarded jealously (from upstarts like Helena) or expended carelessly as he pleases. He thinks of it, indeed, as an analogue to his ancestral ring, which he is ready to barter away to purchase a night's pleasure. The squandering of the ring, Bertram's patrimony embodied in the form most meaningful to him, a concrete emblem of family dignity and feudal worth, marks the low point in his falling away from his true heritage – the low point, and, hence, the turning point, since the fact that he bestows the ring on Helena means that it will return to him with value surcharged. The revelation of it on Diana's finger in the last scene makes public the extent of his offense, exposing the hollowness of the honor in behalf of which he has turned away Helena. Like previous morality heroes, Bertram plunges more deeply into shame with this repetition of his fault, and requires a correspondingly "deeper" intervention of beneficent forces in order to be rescued.

The weakness in this design, as so outlined, is that too much of it remains blueprint. Bertram's progress is diagrammed rather than fully realized poetically, assumed rather than demonstrated. Since we never hear him in soliloquy or meditation, we cannot assess the impact of events on him. From his interchanges with other characters we can draw only sketchy inferences. Even in the scene of Parolles' exposure, a crucial one for Bertram's development, Bertram can react only by calling Parolles a cat – three times. Such an inadequate response to an event of such magnitude robs the episode of much of its proper and legitimate weight. The trouble with Bertram is not, as commentators have complained, that he is "disagreeable," but that he is insufficiently interesting, too defective in nerve-tissue, too blunt in sensibility and wooden in his reactions, to command the attention that the plot would seem to be claiming for him. And this trouble, in turn, would seem to stem from his having been conceived to such an extent as a morality hero of the old-fashioned sort, as a passive creature, more acted on than acting, whose character consists largely of the sum of the pressures converging upon him.

Flanking Bertram stand the opposed forces of Helena and Parolles, the latter serving as evil tempter and agent of mischief. It is Parolles who foments Bertram's discontent at court, suggests flight to him, seconds him in his plan to abandon Helena, and acts as go-between in the attempt to seduce Diana. His name, of course, means "words," and he is above all a *word*-monger, claiming prowess he does not possess in an affected language designed to win admiration from foolish young courtiers. His duty as a soldier suggests his role in the plot: he is the drum, or drummer, the specialist in loud, hollow, booming sounds, the one who incites others to action but is incapable of it himself. That his fall from favor should hinge on a pretended exploit to recover the company drum, and that it should be carried out by means of such artful gibberish and calculated nonsense as he himself has traded in make for a peculiarly fitting poetic justice. Further, Parolles is a fop, much preoccupied with dress and fashion. As the noise of the drum symbolizes his emptiness, so his flashy appearance, and the repeated descriptions of him in terms of his scarves and plumes, signify his superficiality. Unlike Helena, whose worth is inner, Parolles is all outside; his soul, as Lafew warns Bertram, lies in his clothes.

His career forms the main satiric strand in the plot. Parolles is constructed after the model of certain comic characters in Ben Jonson, as an impostor, or poseur, whose mission it is to indulge his affectations for a time, impose them on others, and then, in a climactic scene, be stripped of them and revealed for what he is. In Jonsonian comedy, such characters usually collapse into non-existence and vanish at this point; once they have given themselves away, nothing remains. Shakespeare, characteristically, endows Parolles with a further layer of existence, the bedrock of the irreducible human, to which he reverts after his exposure. His pretenses unmasked, he survives henceforward as "the thing he is," coward and rascal, but a fellow creature, and as such able to enlist in the cause of his survival the caustic old counsellor Lafew.

In Helena, the chief romance character, George Bernard Shaw saw an early instance of the life force, the energy of the race manifesting itself in the feminine drive for procreation. Precisely the active element in Helena has sometimes repelled critics; they have found her "pushing" and "calculating." But it is clear that Shakespeare did not regard her as such. Nor did his source. Giletta of Narbona, in Painter, belongs to a familiar category of folk heroine, the girl who performs difficult or impossible tasks, and is rewarded with the hand of her high-born beloved. In the case of Bertram, Shakespeare underscores the coarseness of Count Beltramo's behavior, and so aggravates the indictment against him. In the case of Helena, he removes the faint traces of disapproval that clung to Giletta in the tale for her presumption in wishing to marry a count, and so mobilizes our sympathies more urgently in her behalf. In addition he chooses to make hers the most fully articulated consciousness in the play, the one whose feelings are projected with most intensity and explored with greatest complexity. Helena is at once Shakespeare's most ardent and most introspective heroine, and her presence in the centre of the design accounts for much of its mood of fervor and impassioned seriousness.

Shakespeare initiates, furthermore, from the outset a contrast between Helena and Bertram, with regard to their relations with their elders, their manner of claiming their birthrights, their notions of honor, and much else. Helena's father, like Bertram's, is dead before the play opens. But whereas the Countess's exhortations stress the fact that Bertram is as yet — in the respects that matter — only potentially his father's son, Helena has already shown herself worthy of her stock; "she derives her honesty and achieves her goodness." She does not hold her heritage, as Bertram does his nobility, as an inert thing. She actualizes it, recreates it, *achieves* it in her daily existence.

Her skill as a physician, which borders on the magical, is the visible emblem of her patrimony, as Bertram's family ring is of his. But where Bertram spends his ring merely to buy an hour's pleasure, and regards himself as in no way committed by the transaction, Helena offers her remedy in a gesture of total engagement, ready to give herself to Bertram if she succeeds, ready to submit to death and torture if she fails. Such a gift, involving as it does her whole being, inevitably falls on stony ground, is misunderstood, and perhaps feared, by one who at this moment is captivated by words and surfaces, and unacquainted with recesses in himself or others.

The sole error Helena makes is in supposing that love can be earned, that she can somehow *deserve* Bertram. And the only way in which her compact with the king resembles Bertram's bargain with Diana is that both are contracts. The one extenuation, hence, that may be allowed Bertram's otherwise inadmissible churlishness is that he is being asked, in effect, to render as a duty, to give as payment, what can only be bestowed freely and spontaneously. Love, like the mercy of which Portia speaks in *The Merchant of Venice*, cannot be wrung or "strained," but drops like rain from heaven. That Helena does not at first see this, or does not see it clearly, constitutes her sole flaw. But it is enough to make her feel she has sinned, offended through "ambitious love," and to prompt her to a penitential pilgrimage. The central part of the play abounds in the ironies of juxtaposition in which Shakespearean drama is always fertile. As we pass back and forth from Florence to Rossillion, as the stage fills and clears, we move from the camp of war, where Bertram declares his hatred of love, to the home of love, where Helena confesses her terror of war. It is not until love and war can in some sense merge, through the agency of the bed trick, that Bertram's combativeness, which appears momentarily victorious, can in fact be subdued by love and turned to creative ends.

What is apt to bother modern readers about the bed trick that resolves the complications is not so much its indelicacy as its inappropriateness. It seems too mechanical an expedient, too remote from the nuances of the situation it is asked to catalyze. The folk tale premise, acceptable enough in folk tale—that two people otherwise wholly different can be indistinguishable in bed (because darkness constitutes a perfect disguise, and sexual intimacy involves recognition only on the bodily level)—seems unacceptable, even shocking, when applied to characters of the individuality of Bertram and Helena. A Bertram who really could not tell Helena from Diana in bed would not belong in a play by Shakespeare at all, nor would a Helena who thought such a deception possible.

Nevertheless the bed trick fosters our sense that events

are moving darkly, that they drift on mysterious currents hidden from the eye of day and reason, that their outcome awaits the touch of forces beyond the characters' control. Such, too, would seem to be the sense of the curious series of "removes" through which Helena must pursue the court before catching up with it: even while actively engaged in her quest, she must await the propitious moment, the conjunction of other forces, to bring her plan to fruition. In her power to call into being the world of her desires, Helena forms a transitional figure between the heroines of earlier Shakespearean comedy — Portia and Rosalind and Viola — who transform their surroundings largely through natural means, and the explicit wielders of supernatural power, the Cerimons and Prosperos, who preside over the frankly miraculous worlds of the late romances.

The finale, strenuously composed though it is, seems somewhere to take a wrong turn. We can understand the need for Bertram to repeat, even compound, his former error, in the manner of the morality hero, as though to illustrate the stubbornness of flesh and blood, the instability of virtue however painfully arrived at. Having scorned Helena for her low birth, Bertram now rejects Diana for her supposed low morality, applying in this case as in that the shallowest measure of lowness. Having frivolously paid out his ancestral ring, he as lightly dismisses the binding claim of the ring accepted in return. Having dishonored his heritage once, in the very act of claiming to defend it, he must do so a second time, and be rescued from himself by the near-miraculous interposition of Helena. What chills us is that the Bertram who perpetrates this fresh offense remains the same Bertram as before — not one capable of feeling a deeper shame when his evasions are exposed, but the same self-willed, self-satisfied adolescent of the earlier scenes, ready to trivialize all of his experience. His behavior, indeed, would seem to contradict the claims made for him on various occasions, that he has changed "almost into another man," that he was "misled" by Parolles, that his "blames" were "high-repented." And again we seem confronted, at a critical moment, with the inadequacy of an older, more schematic form of character portrayal called upon to function in a vastly evolved and elaborated context. Bertram being the pivotal figure of the last scene, the one toward whom all the energy of the plot is now directed, we must believe in the possibility of his change if we are to experience the joyful release decreed by the ending. But that belief is blunted beyond repair by the incompleteness with which he is presented. Hence our slight sense of constriction at the end. The play itself seems unable to summon the note of serenity or confidence. The closing couplet rings with the memory of past bitterness more than the expectation of future joy.

Nevertheless we may feel that the sombre close has its own vibrations, and accords well with the sombre beauty of much of the play. If the unfolding of events has left little space for merriment, it has been visited by moments of brooding fervor, of lofty dignity, a dignity heightened by the gnomic couplets and the formal verses, and able to survive the defective postures of Bertram in the finale. Few moments in drama are as highly charged as Diana's riddle, with its cadence — "And now behold the meaning" — as Helena appears to irradiate the mysteries of the plot with her presence. And few are as affecting as the subsequent recognitions, which in their troubled solemnity foreshadow the profounder harmonies of the late romances.

University of California   JONAS A. BARISH

Note on the text: All's Well That Ends Well was first published in the folio of 1623, with Shakespeare's own draft evidently serving as printer's copy. Although marred by certain misprints and minor irregularities, it is a reasonably good text and has been followed closely in the present edition; all material departures from it have been listed in the Appendix. The folio text is divided into acts corresponding with those in modern editions, but not into scenes. The act-scene division here supplied marginally for reference purposes is that of the Globe text.

All's Well That Ends Well

[Names of the Actors

King of France
Duke of Florence
Bertram, Count of Rossillion
Lafew, an old lord
Parolles, a follower of Bertram
Rinaldo, steward to the Countess of Rossillion
Lavatch, a clown in her household
A Page in her household
Countess of Rossillion, mother of Bertram
Helena, orphaned daughter of the Countess's physician
Widow Capilet, of Florence
Diana, her daughter
Violenta ⎱ neighbors and friends to the Widow
Mariana ⎰
Lords, Attendants, Soldiers, Messengers, etc., French and
  Florentine

Scene
Rossillion, Paris, Florence, Marseilles]

ALL'S WELL THAT ENDS WELL

Enter young Bertram, Count of Rossillion, his Mother   I, i
[the Dowager Countess], and Helena; Lord Lafew — all
in black.

Countess. In delivering my son from me I bury a second
  husband.

Bertram. And I in going, madam, weep o'er my father's
  death anew; but I must attend his majesty's command,
  to whom I am now in ward, evermore in subjection.   5

Lafew. You shall find of the king a husband, madam; you,
  sir, a father. He that so generally is at all times good
  must of necessity hold his virtue to you, whose worthiness would stir it up where it wanted, rather than lack it
  where there is such abundance.   10

Countess. What hope is there of his majesty's amendment?

Lafew. He hath abandoned his physicians, madam; under
  whose practices he hath persecuted time with hope, and
  finds no other advantage in the process but only the losing
  of hope by time.   15

Countess. This young gentlewoman had a father — O, that
  'had,' how sad a passage 'tis — whose skill was almost as

I, i, 5 *to . . . ward* whose ward I now am   7 *generally* to all men   8 *hold*
maintain   9 *wanted* was absent   *lack* be without   13 *persecuted time* painfully persevered in living   17 *passage* phrase (with pun on 'passing away')

great as his honesty; had it stretched so far, would have
made nature immortal, and death should have play for
20 lack of work. Would for the king's sake he were living!
I think it would be the death of the king's disease.

Lafew. How called you the man you speak of, madam?

Countess. He was famous, sir, in his profession, and it was
his great right to be so — Gerard de Narbon.

25 *Lafew.* He was excellent indeed, madam. The king very
lately spoke of him admiringly and mournfully. He was
skillful enough to have lived still, if knowledge could be
set up against mortality.

Bertram. What is it, my good lord, the king languishes of?

30 *Lafew.* A fistula, my lord.

Bertram. I heard not of it before.

Lafew. I would it were not notorious. Was this gentlewoman the daughter of Gerard de Narbon?

Countess. His sole child, my lord, and bequeathed to my
35 overlooking. I have those hopes of her good that her
education promises. Her dispositions she inherits, which
makes fair gifts fairer; for where an unclean mind carries
virtuous qualities, there commendations go with pity —
they are virtues and traitors too. In her they are the
40 better for their simpleness. She derives her honesty and
achieves her goodness.

Lafew. Your commendations, madam, get from her tears.

Countess. 'Tis the best brine a maiden can season her praise
in. The remembrance of her father never approaches her
45 heart but the tyranny of her sorrows takes all livelihood
from her cheek. No more of this, Helena. Go to, no

---

27 *still* forever   35 *overlooking* supervision   38 *virtuous qualities* praise-
worthy skills   *go* are mixed   40 *simpleness* being unmixed with vice
derives inherits   41 *achieves* attains by her own efforts   43 *season* preserve
45 *livelihood* liveliness

more, lest it be rather thought you affect a sorrow than
to have.

Helena. [aside] I do affect a sorrow indeed, but I have it too.

Lafew. Moderate lamentation is the right of the dead, 50
excessive grief the enemy to the living.

Countess. If the living be enemy to the grief, the excess
makes it soon mortal.

Lafew. How understand we that?

Bertram. Madam, I desire your holy wishes. 55

Countess. Be thou blest, Bertram, and succeed thy father
In manners, as in shape. Thy blood and virtue
Contend for empire in thee, and thy goodness
Share with thy birthright. Love all, trust a few,
Do wrong to none. Be able for thine enemy 60
Rather in power than use, and keep thy friend
Under thy own life's key. Be checked for silence,
But never taxed for speech. What heaven more will,
That thee may furnish, and my prayers pluck down,
Fall on thy head! — Farewell, my lord. 65
'Tis an unseasoned courtier. Good my lord,
Advise him.

Lafew.   He cannot want the best
That shall attend his love.

Countess. Heaven bless him! Farewell, Bertram. [Exit.]

Bertram. The best wishes that can be forged in your thoughts 70
be servants to you! [to Helena] Be comfortable to my
mother, your mistress, and make much of her.

Lafew. Farewell, pretty lady. You must hold the credit of
your father.   [Exeunt Bertram and Lafew.]

52–53 *If . . . mortal* if the living restrain their grief, the grief will soon
burn itself out through its own excess 60 *able* a match 61 *in power*
potentially *use* as a matter of habit 61–62 *keep . . . key* defend your
friend's life as you would your own 62 *checked* reproved 63 *taxed for*
speech rebuked for chattering 71 *comfortable* comforting 73 *hold* uphold

75 *Helena.* O, were that all! I think not on my father,
   And these great tears grace his remembrance more
   Than those I shed for him. What was he like?
   I have forgot him. My imagination
   Carries no favor in't but Bertram's.
80 I am undone; there is no living, none,
   If Bertram be away. 'Twere all one
   That I should love a bright particular star
   And think to wed it, he is so above me.
   In his bright radiance and collateral light
85 Must I be comforted, not in his sphere.
   Th' ambition in my love thus plagues itself:
   The hind that would be mated by the lion
   Must die for love. 'Twas pretty, though a plague,
   To see him every hour, to sit and draw
90 His archèd brows, his hawking eye, his curls,
   In our heart's table — heart too capable
   Of every line and trick of his sweet favor.
   But now he's gone, and my idolatrous fancy
   Must sanctify his relics. Who comes here?

Enter Parolles.

95 One that goes with him; I love him for his sake,
   And yet I know him a notorious liar,
   Think him a great way fool, solely a coward.
   Yet these fixed evils sit so fit in him
   That they take place when virtue's steely bones
100 Looks bleak i' th' cold wind; withal, full oft we see

77 *those ... him* i.e. when he died   79 *favor* face   84 *collateral* i.e.
shed from above, from a distance   85 *sphere* the orbit in which he himself moves   90 *hawking* hawklike, sharpsighted   91 *table* drawing-board
capable readily impressed   92 *trick* trait   *favor* face   95 *his* Bertram's
99 *take place* find welcome   99-100 *when ... wind* when virtue looks pur-
itanical and forbidding

34

Cold wisdom waiting on superfluous folly.

Parolles. Save you, fair queen!

Helena. And you, monarch!

Parolles. No.

Helena. And no. 105

Parolles. Are you meditating on virginity?

Helena. Ay. You have some stain of soldier in you; let me ask you a question. Man is enemy to virginity; how may we barricado it against him?

Parolles. Keep him out. 110

Helena. But he assails, and our virginity, though valiant, in the defense yet is weak. Unfold to us some warlike resistance.

Parolles. There is none. Man setting down before you will undermine you and blow you up. 115

Helena. Bless our poor virginity from underminers and blowers-up! Is there no military policy how virgins might blow up men?

Parolles. Virginity being blown down, man will quicklier be blown up; marry, in blowing him down again, with 120 the breach yourselves made you lose your city. It is not politic in the commonwealth of nature to preserve virginity. Loss of virginity is rational increase, and there was never virgin got till virginity was first lost. That you were made of is metal to make virgins. Virginity by 125 being once lost may be ten times found; by being ever

---

101 *waiting on* taking a back seat to, playing second fiddle to *superfluous* i.e. overdressed 107 *stain* tinge 114 *setting down before* besieging 115 *blow you up* (with pun on 'get you with child') 120 *blown up* i.e. 'reinflated' 120-21 *in ... city* in quenching his ardor (by yielding to it) you lose the fortress of your virginity 122 *politic* statesmanlike 123 *rational increase* reasonable rate of population growth 124 *got* begotten *That* that which 126 *may ... found* i.e. may engender ten more virgins

kept it is ever lost. 'Tis too cold a companion. Away with't!

Helena. I will stand for't a little, though therefore I die a
130 virgin.

Parolles. There's little can be said in't; 'tis against the rule of nature. To speak on the part of virginity is to accuse your mothers, which is most infallible disobedience. He that hangs himself is a virgin; virginity murders itself,
135 and should be buried in highways out of all sanctified limit, as a desperate offendress against nature. Virginity breeds mites, much like a cheese, consumes itself to the very paring, and so dies with feeding his own stomach. Besides, virginity is peevish, proud, idle, made of self-
140 love, which is the most inhibited sin in the canon. Keep it not; you cannot choose but lose by't. Out with't! within ten year it will make itself ten, which is a goodly increase, and the principal itself not much the worse. Away with't!

145 *Helena.* How might one do, sir, to lose it to her own liking?

Parolles. Let me see. Marry, ill, to like him that ne'er it likes. 'Tis a commodity will lose the gloss with lying: the longer kept, the less worth. Off with't while 'tis
150 vendible; answer the time of request. Virginity, like an old courtier, wears her cap out of fashion, richly suited,

---

129 *stand for* defend   131 *in't* in its behalf   132 *on the part of* in defense of   133 *infallible* undoubted   135–36 *out ... limit* in unsanctified ground   137 *breeds mites* i.e. breeds its own destruction   138 *feeding ... stomach* maintaining its own pride   140 *inhibited* prohibited   *canon* catalogue of sins   140 *Keep* hoard   141 *Out with't* lend it out at interest   143 *increase* rate of interest   *principal* capital, i.e. the ex-virgin herself   147 *Marry* indeed   147–48 *ill ... likes* one must do ill, and like the man who does not like virginity   148 *lying* lying idle   149 *Off with't* dispose of it   150 *answer ... request* market it while it is still in demand   151 *out of fashion* unfashionably

but unsuitable, just like the brooch and the toothpick,
which wear not now. Your date is better in your pie and
your porridge than in your cheek; and your virginity,
your old virginity, is like one of our French withered   155
pears: it looks ill, it eats drily. Marry, 'tis a withered
pear; it was formerly better; marry, yet 'tis a withered
pear! Will you anything with it?

Helena. Not my virginity yet. . . .

There shall your master have a thousand loves,   160
A mother, and a mistress, and a friend,
A phoenix, captain, and an enemy,
A guide, a goddess, and a sovereign,
A counsellor, a traitress, and a dear;
His humble ambition, proud humility,   165
His jarring concord, and his discord dulcet,
His faith, his sweet disaster; with a world
Of pretty, fond, adoptious christendoms
That blinking Cupid gossips. Now shall he —
I know not what he shall. God send him well!   170
The court's a learning place, and he is one —

Parolles. What one, i' faith?

Helena. That I wish well. 'Tis pity —

Parolles. What's pity?

Helena. That wishing well had not a body in't,   175
    Which might be felt; that we, the poorer born,

151-52 *richly . . . unsuitable* dressed richly but inappropriately 153 *wear
not* are not worn 153-54 *Your . . . cheek* dates (fruit) serve better to
sweeten porridge than to show up (as years) in your face 156 *eats drily*
tastes dry 159 *Not . . . yet* the moment has not come for me to surrender
my virginity (?) (There may be an accidental omission in the text at this
point.) 160-67 *loves . . . disaster* (a series of epithets, similar to those
in much Elizabethan love poetry, used to characterize the beloved)
168 *fond . . . christendoms* foolish adopted nicknames 169 *That . . . gossips*
for which blind Cupid acts as godfather, i.e. inspired by love 171 *learning
place* place of learning, school 175-76 *That . . . felt* that good will were
not something substantial, and in itself effective

Whose baser stars do shut us up in wishes,
Might with effects of them follow our friends,
And show what we alone must think, which never
180 Returns us thanks.

Enter Page.

Page. Monsieur Parolles, my lord calls for you.   *[Exit.]*
Parolles. Little Helen, farewell. If I can remember thee, I
will think of thee at court.
Helena. Monsieur Parolles, you were born under a char-
185 itable star.
Parolles. Under Mars I. *aye*
Helena. I especially think, under Mars.
Parolles. Why under Mars?
Helena. The wars hath so kept you under that you must
190 needs be born under Mars.
Parolles. When he was predominant.
Helena. When he was retrograde, I think rather.
Parolles. Why think you so?
Helena. You go so much backward when you fight.
195 *Parolles.* That's for advantage.
Helena. So is running away when fear proposes the safety.
But the composition that your valor and fear makes in
you is a virtue of a good wing, and I like the wear well.
Parolles. I am so full of businesses I cannot answer thee
200 acutely. I will return perfect courtier, in the which my

177 *Whose ... wishes* whose inferior fortunes confine us to mere wishing
178 *Might ... follow* might actively assist   179–80 *show ... thanks* make
effective (in acts) what we must conceal in our thoughts and hence remain
unthanked for   184 *under* under the astrological influence of   189 *under*
down   191 *predominant* in the ascendant   192 *retrograde* unfavorably dis-
posed, going 'backward' (hence prompting those born under his influence
to run away)   195 *advantage* strategic benefit   197 *composition* mixture
198 *virtue* property *of ... wing* useful for flight *wear* fashion   200
acutely aptly

instruction shall serve to naturalize thee, so thou wilt be
capable of a courtier's counsel, and understand what advice shall thrust upon thee; else thou diest in thine un-
thankfulness, and thine ignorance makes thee away.
Farewell. When thou hast leisure, say thy prayers; when   205
thou hast none, remember thy friends. Get thee a good
husband, and use him as he uses thee. So, farewell. *[Exit.]*
Helena. Our remedies oft in ourselves do lie,
    Which we ascribe to heaven. The fated sky
    Gives us free scope; only doth backward pull   210
    Our slow designs when we ourselves are dull.
    What power is it which mounts my love so high?
    That makes me see, and cannot feed mine eye?
    The mightiest space in fortune nature brings
    To join like likes, and kiss like native things.   215
    Impossible be strange attempts to those
    That weigh their pains in sense, and do suppose
    What hath been cannot be. Who ever strove
    To show her merit that did miss her love?
    The king's disease — my project may deceive me,   220
    But my intents are fixed, and will not leave me. *[Exit.]*

201 *naturalize* familiarize *so if* 202 *capable of* able to profit from
204 *makes thee away* destroys you 205–6 *when . . . friends* i.e. don't remember them at all 207 *use* treat 209 *fated* fateful 213 *makes . . .
eye* enables me to appreciate Bertram without satisfying my desire to see
him (?) 214–15 *The . . . things* nature causes things of the widest diversity
in station to unite and embrace as though born equals 217 *That . . . sense*
who count the cost and measure their discomforts

I, ii   *Flourish cornets. Enter the King of France with letters, and*
        divers Attendants.

   King. The Florentines and Senoys are by th' ears,
      Have fought with equal fortune, and continue
      A braving war.
   1. Lord.   So 'tis reported, sir.
   King. Nay, 'tis most credible. We here receive it
5   A certainty vouched from our cousin Austria,
      With caution, that the Florentine will move us
      For speedy aid; wherein our dearest friend
      Prejudicates the business, and would seem
      To have us make denial.
   1. Lord.   His love and wisdom,
10   Approved so to your majesty, may plead
      For amplest credence.
   King.   He hath armed our answer,
      And Florence is denied before he comes.
      Yet, for our gentlemen that mean to see
      The Tuscan service, freely have they leave
      To stand on either part.
15 *2. Lord.*   It well may serve
      A nursery to our gentry, who are sick
      For breathing and exploit.
   King.   What's he comes here?

        Enter Bertram, Lafew, and Parolles.

   1. Lord. It is the Count Rossillion, my good lord,
      Young Bertram.

I, ii, 1 *Senoys* Sienese   *by th' ears* at war   3 *braving* defiant   5 *cousin*
fellow monarch   6 *move* petition   8 *Prejudicates* prejudges   10 *Approved*
proved   15 *stand* serve   *part* side   16 *nursery* training-ground   17 *breath-*
ing exercise

King.   Youth, thou bear'st thy father's face.
   Frank nature, rather curious than in haste,   20
   Hath well composed thee. Thy father's moral parts
   Mayst thou inherit too! Welcome to Paris.
Bertram. My thanks and duty are your majesty's.
King. I would I had that corporal soundness now
   As when thy father and myself in friendship   25
   First tried our soldiership. He did look far
   Into the service of the time, and was
   Discipled of the bravest. He lasted long,
   But on us both did haggish age steal on,
   And wore us out of act. It much repairs me   30
   To talk of your good father; in his youth
   He had the wit which I can well observe
   To-day in our young lords; but they may jest
   Till their own scorn return to them unnoted
   Ere they can hide their levity in honor.   35
   So like a courtier, contempt nor bitterness
   Were in his pride, or sharpness. If they were,
   His equal had awaked them, and his honor,
   Clock to itself, knew the true minute when
   Exception bid him speak, and at this time   40
   His tongue obeyed his hand. Who were below him
   He used as creatures of another place,
   And bowed his eminent top to their low ranks,
   Making them proud of his humility,

20 *Frank* liberal *curious* careful 21 *composed* constructed 26–27 *did
. . . time* deeply understood the business of war 27–28 *was . . . bravest*
numbered the bravest among his disciples 30 *wore . . . act* reduced us
to inaction 34 *unnoted* unnoticed 35 *hide . . . honor* subordinate their
frivolity to their dignity 39 *Clock to itself* 'self-regulating' *true* exact
40 *Exception* disapproval 41 *obeyed his hand* said only what his hand
(i.e. his sword) could back up *Who* those who 42 *another place* i.e. a
higher rank

45   In their poor praise he humbled. Such a man
Might be a copy to these younger times,
Which, followed well, would demonstrate them now
But goers backward.

Bertram.   His good remembrance, sir,
Lies richer in your thoughts than on his tomb.

50   So in approof lives not his epitaph
As in your royal speech.

King. Would I were with him! He would always say —
Methinks I hear him now; his plausive words
He scattered not in ears, but grafted them

55   To grow there, and to bear — 'Let me not live' —
This his good melancholy oft began,
On the catastrophe and heel of pastime,
When it was out — 'Let me not live,' quoth he,
'After my flame lacks oil, to be the snuff

60   Of younger spirits, whose apprehensive senses
All but new things disdain; whose judgments are
Mere fathers of their garments; whose constancies
Expire before their fashions.' This he wished.
I, after him, do after him wish too,

65   Since I nor wax nor honey can bring home,
I quickly were dissolvèd from my hive,
To give some laborers room.

2. Lord.   You're loved, sir.
They that least lend it you shall lack you first.

---

45 *In ... humbled* he graciously condescended to the humble by praising them(?)   48 *goers backward* laggards   50–51 *So ... As* the tribute on his tomb is nowhere better verified than   53 *plausive* plausible   54 *scattered ... grafted* did not strew superficially among his hearers, but planted deeply   57 *catastrophe and heel* end and completion   58 *it* i.e. pastime out over   59 *snuff* charred wicks hindering free burning, hence impediment   60 *apprehensive* keen   61–62 *whose ... garments* whose minds are wholly taken up with devising new fashions   66 *dissolvèd* separated   68 *lend it you* acknowledge it   *lack* miss

King. I fill a place, I know't. How long is't, count,
   Since the physician at your father's died?   70
   He was much famed.
Bertram.   Some six months since, my lord.
King. If he were living, I would try him yet.
   Lend me an arm. The rest have worn me out
   With several applications; nature and sickness
   Debate it at their leisure. Welcome, count;   75
   My son 's no dearer.
Bertram.   Thank your majesty.
                              Exeunt. Flourish.

Enter Countess, Steward, and [Lavatch, a] Clown.   I, iii

Countess. I will now hear. What say you of this gentlewoman?
Steward. Madam, the care I have had to even your content
   I wish might be found in the calendar of my past endeavors; for then we wound our modesty, and make foul   5
   the clearness of our deservings, when of ourselves we
   publish them.
Countess. What does this knave here? Get you gone,
   sirrah. The complaints I have heard of you I do not all
   believe. 'Tis my slowness that I do not; for I know you 10
   lack not folly to commit them, and have ability enough
   to make such knaveries yours.
Lavatch. 'Tis not unknown to you, madam, I am a poor
   fellow.
Countess. Well, sir.   15

74 *several applications* various treatments   I, iii, 3 *even your content* satisfy
your wishes   4–5 *calendar . . . endeavors* record of my past service   6 *clearness* luster   *deservings* deserts   7 *publish* make known

Lavatch. No, madam, 'tis not so well that I am poor,
   though many of the rich are damned; but if I may have
   your ladyship's good will to go to the world, Isbel the
   woman and I will do as we may.

20 *Countess.* Wilt thou needs be a beggar?

Lavatch. I do beg your good will in this case.

Countess. In what case?

Lavatch. In Isbel's case and mine own. Service is no heritage,
   and I think I shall never have the blessing of God till I

25   have issue o' my body; for they say barnes are blessings.

Countess. Tell me thy reason why thou wilt marry.

Lavatch. My poor body, madam, requires it; I am driven
   on by the flesh; and he must needs go that the devil drives.

Countess. Is this all your worship's reason?

30 *Lavatch.* Faith, madam, I have other holy reasons, such as
   they are.

Countess. May the world know them?

Lavatch. I have been, madam, a wicked creature, as you
   and all flesh and blood are, and indeed I do marry that

35   I may repent.

Countess. Thy marriage, sooner than thy wickedness.

Lavatch. I am out o' friends, madam, and I hope to have
   friends for my wife's sake.

Countess. Such friends are thine enemies, knave.

40 *Lavatch.* Y'are shallow, madam, in great friends; for the
   knaves come to do that for me which I am aweary of.
   He that ears my land spares my team and gives me leave
   to in the crop; if I be his cuckold, he's my drudge. He
   that comforts my wife is the cherisher of my flesh and

45   blood; he that cherishes my flesh and blood loves my
   flesh and blood; he that loves my flesh and blood is my

18 *go ... world* get married   25 *barnes* children   37 *out o'* without   40
shallow ... in superficial ... in judging   42 *ears* ploughs   43 *in* harvest

44

friend: ergo, he that kisses my wife is my friend. If men
could be contented to be what they are, there were no
fear in marriage; for young Charbon the puritan and
old Poysam the papist, howsome'er their hearts are sev-   50
ered in religion, their heads are both one — they may
jowl horns together like any deer i' th' herd.

Countess. Wilt thou ever be a foul-mouthed and calum-
nious knave?

Lavatch. A prophet I, madam, and I speak the truth the   55
next way:

    For I the ballad will repeat,
      Which men full true shall find:
    Your marriage comes by destiny,
      Your cuckoo sings by kind.   60

Countess. Get you gone, sir. I'll talk with you more anon.

Steward. May it please you, madam, that he bid Helen come
to you. Of her I am to speak.

Countess. Sirrah, tell my gentlewoman I would speak with
her — Helen I mean.   65

Lavatch. 'Was this fair face the cause,' quoth she,
    'Why the Grecians sackèd Troy?
    Fond done, done fond,
      Was this King Priam's joy?'
    With that she sighèd as she stood,   70
    With that she sighèd as she stood,
      And gave this sentence then:
    'Among nine bad if one be good,
    Among nine bad if one be good,
      There's yet one good in ten.'   75

48 *what they are* i.e. cuckolds   49 *Charbon* 'chair bonne,' i.e. meat-eater
50 *Poysam* 'poisson,' i.e. fish-eater   50–51 *severed* divided   51 *both
one* exactly alike   52 *jowl* knock   *deer . . . herd* horned beasts, i.e. cuckolds
56 *next* nearest   60 *kind* nature   66 *she* possibly Hecuba, widow of
Priam   68 *Fond* foolishly   69 *Priam* king of Troy

45

Countess. What, one good in ten? You corrupt the song, sirrah.

Lavatch. One good woman in ten, madam, which is a purifying o' th' song. Would God would serve the world
80 so all the year! We'd find no fault with the tithe-woman, if I were the parson. One in ten, quoth 'a? An we might have a good woman born but or every blazing star, or at an earthquake, 'twould mend the lottery well; a man may draw his heart out ere 'a pluck one.

85 *Countess.* You'll be gone, sir knave, and do as I command you.

Lavatch. That man should be at woman's command, and yet no hurt done! Though honesty be no puritan, yet it will do no hurt; it will wear the surplice of humility
90 over the black gown of a big heart. I am going, forsooth. The business is for Helen to come hither.   *Exit.*

Countess. Well now.

Steward. I know, madam, you love your gentlewoman entirely.

95 *Countess.* Faith, I do. Her father bequeathed her to me, and she herself, without other advantage, may lawfully make title to as much love as she finds. There is more owing her than is paid, and more shall be paid her than she'll demand.

100 *Steward.* Madam, I was very late more near her than I

---

76 *corrupt the song* (the song presumably found one *bad* in ten; the clown reverses the proportions)   80–81 *We'd . . . parson* one good woman in ten (*tithe-woman*) ought to satisfy the parson as well as one pig in ten   81 *An* if   82 *or . . . or* either . . . or   *blazing star* new star, or comet   83 *mend the lottery* improve the existing odds   84 *pluck one* draw a good woman (in the lottery of marriage)   88 *honesty* chastity   88–89 *wear . . . heart* conform to ecclesiastical rules by wearing the surplice, but remain inwardly rebellious by wearing the puritan black gown underneath   96 *without other advantage* other claims apart   96–97 *make title to* claim

think she wished me; alone she was, and did commu-
nicate to herself her own words to her own ears. She
thought, I dare vow for her, they touched not any
stranger sense. Her matter was, she loved your son.
Fortune, she said, was no goddess, that had put such 105
difference betwixt their two estates; Love no god, that
would not extend his might, only where qualities were
level; Dian no queen of virgins, that would suffer her
poor knight surprised without rescue in the first assault,
or ransom afterward. This she delivered in the most 110
bitter touch of sorrow that e'er I heard virgin exclaim in,
which I held my duty speedily to acquaint you withal,
sithence, in the loss that may happen, it concerns you
something to know it.

Countess. You have discharged this honestly; keep it to 115
yourself. Many likelihoods informed me of this before,
which hung so tottering in the balance that I could
neither believe nor misdoubt. Pray you leave me; stall
this in your bosom; and I thank you for your honest
care. I will speak with you further anon.   *Exit Steward.* 120

Enter Helena.

Even so it was with me when I was young.
  If ever we are nature's, these are ours. This thorn
Doth to our rose of youth rightly belong;
  Our blood to us, this to our blood is born.
It is the show and seal of nature's truth,   125
Where love's strong passion is impressed in youth.
By our remembrances of days foregone,

103–4 *touched . . . sense* could not be overheard by anyone   107–8 *qualities were level* social rank was equal   111 *touch* note   113 *sithence* since
114 *something* somewhat   122 *these* i.e. pangs of love   124 *blood* natural
instincts

Such were our faults, or then we thought them none.
Her eye is sick on't; I observe her now.
Helena. What is your pleasure, madam?
130 *Countess.*   You know, Helen,
I am a mother to you.
Helena. Mine honorable mistress.
Countess.   Nay, a mother.
Why not a mother? When I said 'a mother,'
Methought you saw a serpent. What's in 'mother'
135 That you start at it? I say I am your mother,
And put you in the catalogue of those
That were enwombèd mine. 'Tis often seen
Adoption strives with nature, and choice breeds
A native slip to us from foreign seeds.
140 You ne'er oppressed me with a mother's groan,
Yet I express to you a mother's care.
God's mercy, maiden, does it curd thy blood
To say I am thy mother? What's the matter,
That this distemperèd messenger of wet,
145 The many-colored Iris, rounds thine eye?
Why? that you are my daughter?
Helena.   That I am not.
Countess. I say I am your mother.
Helena.   Pardon, madam.
The Count Rossillion cannot be my brother:
I am from humble, he from honorèd name;
150 No note upon my parents, his all noble.
My master, my dear lord he is, and I

---

128 *or ... none* or, rather, in those days we did not think them faults
129 *on't* with it   138 *strives* competes in strength of love   138–39 *choice ...
seeds* by adoption we make wholly our own what was originally foreign
144 *distemperèd* disordered   *messenger of wet* tear   145 *Iris* rainbow   *rounds*
makes round   150 *note* mark of distinction   *parents* kinsmen

His servant live and will his vassal die.
He must not be my brother.
Countess.   Nor I your mother?
Helena. You are my mother, madam. Would you were —
So that my lord your son were not my brother —   155
Indeed my mother! or were you both our mothers,
I care no more for than I do for heaven,
So I were not his sister. Can 't no other,
But I your daughter, he must be my brother?
Countess. Yes, Helen, you might be my daughter-in-law.   160
God shield you mean it not! 'daughter' and 'mother'
So strive upon your pulse. What, pale again?
My fear hath catched your fondness. Now I see
The myst'ry of your loneliness, and find
Your salt tears' head. Now to all sense 'tis gross: 165
You love my son. Invention is ashamed,
Against the proclamation of thy passion,
To say thou dost not. Therefore tell me true;
But tell me then, 'tis so; for look, thy cheeks
Confess it, t' one to th' other, and thine eyes   170
See it so grossly shown in thy behaviors
That in their kind they speak it. Only sin
And hellish obstinacy tie thy tongue,
That truth should be suspected. Speak, is't so?
If it be so, you have wound a goodly clew;   175
If it be not, forswear't; howe'er, I charge thee,
As heaven shall work in me for thine avail,
To tell me truly.

156 *both our mothers* mother of us both   163 *fondness* sentimental weakness   165 *head* source   *gross* evident   166 *Invention* fabrication of excuses   171 *grossly* openly   172 *in their kind* after their nature, i.e. by weeping   174 *That . . . suspected* in order to cast suspicion on the truth   175 *wound . . . clew* snarled things up handsomely   176 *forswear't* deny it   177 *avail* benefit

Helena.   Good madam, pardon me.

Countess. Do you love my son?

Helena.   Your pardon, noble mistress!

Countess. Love you my son?

180 *Helena.*   Do not you love him, madam?

Countess. Go not about; my love hath in't a bond
Whereof the world takes note. Come, come, disclose
The state of your affection, for your passions
Have to the full appeached.

Helena.   Then I confess

185   Here on my knee before high heaven and you,
That before you, and next unto high heaven,
I love your son.
My friends were poor but honest; so's my love.
Be not offended, for it hurts not him

190   That he is loved of me. I follow him not
By any token of presumptuous suit,
Nor would I have him till I do deserve him;
Yet never know how that desert should be.
I know I love in vain, strive against hope;

195   Yet in this captious and intenible sieve
I still pour in the waters of my love
And lack not to lose still. Thus, Indian-like,
Religious in mine error, I adore
The sun that looks upon his worshipper

200   But knows of him no more. My dearest madam,
Let not your hate encounter with my love,
For loving where you do; but if yourself,
Whose agèd honor cites a virtuous youth,

181 *Go not about* don't beat about the bush   184 *appeached* informed
against you   195 *captious* capacious, and deceptive   *intenible* unretentive
196 *still* constantly   197 *lack ... still* have an abundance, to continue
pouring out and losing   *Indian-like* idolatrously   201 *encounter with* oppose
itself to   203 *cites* betokens

Did ever in so true a flame of liking,
Wish chastely and love dearly, that your Dian   205
Was both herself and Love, O, then give pity
To her whose state is such that cannot choose
But lend and give where she is sure to lose;
That seeks not to find that her search implies,
But, riddle-like, lives sweetly where she dies.   210

Countess. Had you not lately an intent – speak truly –
To go to Paris?

Helena.   Madam, I had.

Countess.   Wherefore? Tell true.

Helena. I will tell truth, by grace itself I swear:
You know my father left me some prescriptions
Of rare and proved effects, such as his reading   215
And manifest experience had collected
For general sovereignty; and that he willed me
In heedfull'st reservation to bestow them,
As notes whose faculties inclusive were
More than they were in note. Amongst the rest   220
There is a remedy, approved, set down,
To cure the desperate languishings whereof
The king is rendered lost.

Countess.   This was your motive
For Paris, was it? Speak.

Helena. My lord your son made me to think of this;   225
Else Paris, and the medicine, and the king
Had from the conversation of my thoughts
Happily been absent then.

205 *that* so that   206 *both . . . Love* i.e. both chaste and passionate   209 *that*
what   210 *riddle-like* paradoxically   217 *For general sovereignty* as
master remedies   218 *In . . . them* to reserve them carefully for special
uses   219–20 *As . . . note* as prescriptions more potent than generally
recognized   221 *approved* tested   223 *rendered lost* reported incurable
227 *conversation* interchange   228 *Happily* haply, perchance

Countess.   But think you, Helen,
　　　If you should tender your supposèd aid,
230　He would receive it? He and his physicians
　　　Are of a mind: he, that they cannot help him;
　　　They, that they cannot help. How shall they credit
　　　A poor unlearnèd virgin, when the schools,
　　　Embowelled of their doctrine, have left off
　　　The danger to itself?
235 *Helena.*   There's something in't
　　　More than my father's skill, which was the great'st
　　　Of his profession, that his good receipt
　　　Shall for my legacy be sanctified
　　　By th' luckiest stars in heaven; and would your honor
240　But give me leave to try success, I'd venture
　　　The well-lost life of mine on his grace's cure
　　　By such a day and hour.
Countess.   Dost thou believe't?
Helena. Ay, madam, knowingly.
Countess. Why, Helen, thou shalt have my leave and love,
245　Means and attendants, and my loving greetings
　　　To those of mine in court. I'll stay at home
　　　And pray God's blessing into thy attempt.
　　　Be gone to-morrow, and be sure of this,
　　　What I can help thee to, thou shalt not miss.   *Exeunt.*

229 *tender* offer 233 *schools* medical faculties 234 *Embowelled ... doctrine* depleted of their knowledge 234–35 *left ... itself* abandoned the disease to its course 237 *that* whereby *receipt* prescription 241 *well-lost* i.e. in such a cause 243 *knowingly* with full knowledge

Enter the King with divers young Lords taking leave for the   II, i
    Florentine war; [Bertram] Count Rossillion, and Parolles.
    Flourish cornets.

King. Farewell, young lords; these warlike principles
    Do not throw from you. And you, my lords, farewell.
    Share the advice betwixt you; if both gain all,
    The gift doth stretch itself as 'tis received,
    And is enough for both.
1. Lord.   'Tis our hope, sir,   5
    After well-ent'red soldiers, to return
    And find your grace in health.
King. No, no, it cannot be. And yet my heart
    Will not confess he owes the malady
    That doth my life besiege. Farewell, young lords.   10
    Whether I live or die, be you the sons
    Of worthy Frenchmen. Let Higher Italy
    (Those bated that inherit but the fall
    Of the last monarchy) see that you come
    Not to woo honor, but to wed it, when   15
    The bravest questant shrinks: find what you seek,
    That fame may cry you loud. I say, farewell.
2. Lord. Health at your bidding serve your majesty!
King. Those girls of Italy, take heed of them.
    They say our French lack language to deny   20
    If they demand; beware of being captives
    Before you serve.
Both.   Our hearts receive your warnings.

II, i, 3–5 *if ... both* if both groups of you follow all my advice, my gift
will be that much ampler, and will serve for both   6 *After ... soldiers*
after making a worthy debut as soldiers   9 *owes* owns   13–14 *Those ...
monarchy* except those who are only heirs to a fallen empire (?)   15 *woo*
i.e. flirt with   *wed* i.e. possess   16 *questant* seeker   17 *cry* proclaim
21 *captives* i.e. to love

King. Farewell. *[to Attendants]* Come hither to me.

                                    [Exit, led by Attendants.]

1. Lord. O my sweet lord, that you will stay behind us!

Parolles. 'Tis not his fault, the spark.

25 *2. Lord.*   O, 'tis brave wars!

Parolles. Most admirable. I have seen those wars.

Bertram. I am commanded here and kept a coil with
    'Too young,' and 'The next year,' and ' 'Tis too early.'

Parolles. An thy mind stand to't, boy, steal away bravely.

30 *Bertram.* I shall stay here the forehorse to a smock,
    Creaking my shoes on the plain masonry,
    Till honor be bought up, and no sword worn
    But one to dance with. By heaven, I'll steal away!

1. Lord. There's honor in the theft.

Parolles.   Commit it, count.

35 *2. Lord.* I am your accessary; and so farewell.

Bertram. I grow to you, and our parting is a tortured
    body.

1. Lord. Farewell, captain.

2. Lord. Sweet Monsieur Parolles!

40 *Parolles.* Noble heroes, my sword and yours are kin. Good
    sparks and lustrous, a word, good metals: you shall find
    in the regiment of the Spinii one Captain Spurio, with
    his cicatrice, an emblem of war, here on his sinister cheek.
    It was this very sword entrenched it; say to him I live,
45   and observe his reports for me.

1. Lord. We shall, noble captain.

Parolles. Mars dote on you for his novices!

                                        [Exeunt Lords.]

---

25 *spark* elegant young man 27 *kept a coil* fussed over 29 *An* if 30 *forehorse* leading horse *smock* woman 31 *plain masonry* level palace floors (instead of the rough battlefield) 36 *grow to* grow deeply attached to 36–37 *a tortured body* like a body being torn apart 41 *metals* 'blades' 43 *sinister* left

What will ye do?

[Enter the King, led back to his chair by Attendants.]

Bertram. Stay — the king.

Parolles. Use a more spacious ceremony to the noble lords, 50
you have restrained yourself within the list of too cold an
adieu. Be more expressive to them; for they wear themselves in the cap of the time; there do muster true gait,
eat, speak, and move under the influence of the most
received star; and though the devil lead the measure, 55
such are to be followed. After them, and take a more
dilated farewell.

Bertram. And I will do so.

Parolles. Worthy fellows, and like to prove most sinewy
swordmen.   *Exeunt [Bertram and Parolles].* 60

Enter Lafew.

Lafew. *[Kneels.]* Pardon, my lord, for me and for my tidings.

King. I'll fee thee to stand up.

Lafew. *[Rises.]* Then here's a man stands that has brought
his pardon.

I would you had kneeled, my lord, to ask me mercy,
And that at my bidding you could so stand up.   65

King. I would I had, so I had broke thy pate
And asked thee mercy for't.

Lafew.   Good faith, across!
But, my good lord, 'tis thus: will you be cured
Of your infirmity?

50 *spacious* elaborate   51 *list* bounds   52 *expressive* unreserved
52–53 *wear ... time* shine in the fashionable world   53 *muster true gait*
set the right pace   54–55 *move ... star* conform to the reigning fashions
55 *measure* dance   56 *such* such leaders   57 *dilated* extended   62 *fee*
pay   67 *across* wide of the mark (referring to the king's attempt at a
jest in ll. 66–67)

   King.   No.
   Lafew.   O, will you eat
70   No grapes, my royal fox? Yes, but you will
     My noble grapes, an if my royal fox
     Could reach them. I have seen a medicine
     That's able to breathe life into a stone,
     Quicken a rock, and make you dance canary
75   With sprightly fire and motion; whose simple touch
     Is powerful to araise King Pepin, nay,
     To give great Charlemain a pen in 's hand,
     And write to her a love-line.
   King.   What 'her' is this?
   Lafew. Why, Doctor She! My lord, there's one arrived,
80   If you will see her. Now by my faith and honor,
     If seriously I may convey my thoughts
     In this my light deliverance, I have spoke
     With one that in her sex, her years, profession,
     Wisdom and constancy, hath amazed me more
85   Than I dare blame my weakness. Will you see her,
     For that is her demand, and know her business?
     That done, laugh well at me.
   King.   Now, good Lafew,
     Bring in the admiration, that we with thee
     May spend our wonder too, or take off thine
     By wond'ring how thou took'st it.
90 *Lafew.*   Nay, I'll fit you,
     And not be all day neither.   *[Exit.]*
   King. Thus he his special nothing ever prologues.

---

71 *an if* if   74 *Quicken* bring to life   *canary* lively Spanish dance
76 *araise* raise up   *Pepin* eighth-century French king   82 *light deliverance*
frivolous delivery   84–85 *more . . . weakness* more than I can account
for by blaming my senility   88 *admiration* wonder   89 *spend* utter   *take
off* dispel, remove   90 *took'st* came by   92 *special nothing* particular
trifles

Enter [Lafew, with] Helena.

Lafew. Nay, come your ways.
King.   This haste hath wings indeed.
Lafew. Nay, come your ways;
   This is his majesty; say your mind to him.   95
   A traitor you do look like, but such traitors
   His majesty seldom fears. I am Cressid's uncle,
   That dare leave two together. Fare you well.   *Exit.*
King. Now, fair one, does your business follow us?
Helena. Ay, my good lord.   100
   Gerard de Narbon was my father;
   In what he did profess, well-found.
King.   I knew him.
Helena. The rather will I spare my praises towards him;
   Knowing him is enough. On 's bed of death
   Many receipts he gave me, chiefly one,   105
   Which as the dearest issue of his practice
   And of his old experience th' only darling,
   He bade me store up as a triple eye,
   Safer than mine own two, more dear; I have so;
   And hearing your high majesty is touched   110
   With that malignant cause wherein the honor
   Of my dear father's gift stands chief in power,
   I come to tender it and my appliance,
   With all bound humbleness.
King.   We thank you, maiden;
   But may not be so credulous of cure,   115

97 *Cressid's uncle* Pandarus, hence pander   102 *In . . . well-found* found to
be good at his profession, medicine   105 *receipts* prescriptions   106 *dearest
issue* most treasured product   107 *of . . . darling* the only formula that
remained precious after repeated trial   108 *triple* third   111 *cause* disease
111–12 *wherein . . . power* for which my father's remedy is most effective
113 *tender* offer   *appliance* treatment   114 *bound* dutiful

When our most learnèd doctors leave us, and
The congregated college have concluded
That laboring art can never ransom nature
From her inaidable estate. I say we must not
120 So stain our judgment, or corrupt our hope,
To prostitute our past-cure malady
To empirics, or to dissever so
Our great self and our credit, to esteem
A senseless help, when help past sense we deem.
125 *Helena.* My duty then shall pay me for my pains.
I will no more enforce mine office on you,
Humbly entreating from your royal thoughts
A modest one, to bear me back again.
King. I cannot give thee less, to be called grateful.
130 Thou thought'st to help me, and such thanks I give
As one near death to those that wish him live.
But what at full I know, thou know'st no part,
I knowing all my peril, thou no art.
Helena. What I can do can do no hurt to try,
135 Since you set up your rest 'gainst remedy.
He that of greatest works is finisher
Oft does them by the weakest minister.
So holy writ in babes hath judgment shown
When judges have been babes; great floods have flown
140 From simple sources, and great seas have dried
When miracles have by the greatest been denied.

116 *leave* give up for dead   117 *congregated college* conclave of physicians   118 *art* medicine   119 *inaidable estate* condition of hopelessness
120 *corrupt our hope* hope foolishly   122 *empirics* quacks   122–23 *dissever
... credit* divorce our greatness from our reputation, i.e. behave in an
unkingly manner   123 *esteem* value   124 *senseless* irrational   *past sense*
unreasonable   126 *office* function   128 *A modest one* a belief in my good
intentions and natural modesty   135 *set ... rest* are resolved at all cost
139 *babes* i.e. helpless, foolish   140 *simple* insignificant

Oft expectation fails, and most oft there
Where most it promises; and oft it hits
Where hope is coldest and despair most fits.

King. I must not hear thee; fare thee well, kind maid. 145
Thy pains, not used, must by thyself be paid;
Proffers not took reap thanks for their reward.

Helena. Inspirèd merit so by breath is barred.
It is not so with Him that all things knows
As 'tis with us that square our guess by shows; 150
But most it is presumption in us, when
The help of heaven we count the act of men.
Dear sir, to my endeavors give consent;
Of heaven, not me, make an experiment.
I am not an impostor, that proclaim 155
Myself against the level of mine aim;
But know I think, and think I know most sure,
My art is not past power, nor you past cure.

King. Art thou so confident? Within what space
Hop'st thou my cure?

Helena.   The great'st grace lending grace, 160
Ere twice the horses of the sun shall bring
Their fiery torcher his diurnal ring,
Ere twice in murk and occidental damp
Moist Hesperus hath quenched her sleepy lamp,
Or four and twenty times the pilot's glass 165
Hath told the thievish minutes how they pass,
What is infirm from your sound parts shall fly,
Health shall live free, and sickness freely die.

143 *hits* succeeds 148 *Inspirèd* divinely inspired *so* thus *breath* words
150 *square ... shows* rule our opinions by appearances 155–56 *that ...
aim* who boasts of what he knows he cannot do 162 *torcher* torchbearer
diurnal ring daily round 163 *occidental* of sunset 164 *Hesperus* evening
star *her* (since the evening star is in fact the planet Venus) 165 *glass*
hourglass

King. Upon thy certainty and confidence
　　 What dar'st thou venture?

170 *Helena.*　　　　　　　　　 Tax of impudence,
　　 A strumpet's boldness, a divulgèd shame
　　 Traduced by odious ballads; my maiden's name
　　 Seared otherwise; nay, worse of worst, extended
　　 With vilest torture let my life be ended.

175 *King.* Methinks in thee some blessèd spirit doth speak
　　 His powerful sound within an organ weak;
　　 And what impossibility would slay
　　 In common sense, sense saves another way.
　　 Thy life is dear, for all that life can rate

180　 Worth name of life in thee hath estimate:
　　 Youth, beauty, wisdom, courage — all
　　 That happiness and prime can happy call.
　　 Thou this to hazard needs must intimate
　　 Skill infinite, or monstrous desperate.

185　 Sweet practiser, thy physic I will try,
　　 That ministers thine own death if I die.

Helena. If I break time or flinch in property
　　 Of what I spoke, unpitied let me die,
　　 And well deserved; not helping, death's my fee.

190　 But if I help, what do you promise me?

King. Make thy demand.

Helena.　　　　　　　　 But will you make it even?

King. Ay, by my sceptre and my hopes of heaven.

Helena. Then shalt thou give me with thy kingly hand
　　 What husband in thy power I will command.

170 *Tax* charge 171 *divulgèd* publicly proclaimed 173 *otherwise* in other
ways as well *extended* stretched out, racked 177–78 *what ... way* what
common sense would regard as impossible, a higher sense can believe
180 *estimate* value 182 *prime* youth 185 *practiser* practitioner *physic*
medicine 187 *break time* fail to perform in the stipulated time *flinch in
property* fall short in the particulars 191 *make it even* match it

Exempted be from me the arrogance   195
To choose from forth the royal blood of France,
My low and humble name to propagate
With any branch or image of thy state;
But such a one, thy vassal, whom I know
Is free for me to ask, thee to bestow.   200
King. Here is my hand. The premises observed,
Thy will by my performance shall be served.
So make the choice of thy own time; for I,
Thy resolved patient, on thee still rely.
More should I question thee, and more I must,   205
Though more to know could not be more to trust –
From whence thou cam'st, how tended on – but rest
Unquestioned welcome, and undoubted blest.
Give me some help here, ho! – If thou proceed
As high as word, my deed shall match thy deed.   210

Flourish. Exeunt.

Enter Countess and [Lavatch, the] Clown.   II, ii

Countess. Come on, sir, I shall now put you to the height
of your breeding.

Lavatch. I will show myself highly fed and lowly taught.
I know my business is but to the court.

Countess. To the court? Why, what place make you special, 5
when you put off that with such contempt? But to the
court?

Lavatch. Truly, madam, if God have lent a man any man-

---

204 *still* always II, ii, 1 *put ... height* test the extent 3 *highly ...*
taught i.e. like a rich man's son, overfed and underdisciplined 5 *make*
consider 6 *put off* dismiss

61

ners, he may easily put it off at court: he that cannot
10 make a leg, put off 's cap, kiss his hand, and say nothing,
has neither leg, hands, lip, nor cap; and indeed such a
fellow, to say precisely, were not for the court. But for
me, I have an answer will serve all men.

Countess. Marry, that's a bountiful answer that fits all
15 questions.

Lavatch. It is like a barber's chair that fits all buttocks – the
pin-buttock, the quatch-buttock, the brawn-buttock, or
any buttock.

Countess. Will your answer serve fit to all questions?

20 *Lavatch.* As fit as ten groats is for the hand of an attorney,
as your French crown for your taffety punk, as Tib's
rush for Tom's forefinger, as a pancake for Shrove
Tuesday, a morris for May-day, as the nail to his hole, the
cuckold to his horn, as a scolding quean to a wrangling
25 knave, as the nun's lip to the friar's mouth; nay, as the
pudding to his skin.

Countess. Have you, I say, an answer of such fitness for all
questions?

Lavatch. From below your duke to beneath your con-
30 stable, it will fit any question.

Countess. It must be an answer of most monstrous size
that must fit all demands.

Lavatch. But a trifle neither, in good faith, if the learned
should speak truth of it. Here it is, and all that belongs
35 to't: ask me if I am a courtier; it shall do you no harm
to learn.

---

10 *leg* respectful bow 17 *quatch* fat 20 *ten groats* (the attorney's usual
fee) 21 *French crown* syphilis (with pun on *crown* = a coin) *taffety
punk* finely dressed strumpet 21–22 *Tib's rush* country wench's rush ring
22–23 *Shrove Tuesday* pre-Lenten holiday when quantities of pancakes
were consumed 23 *morris* country dance 24 *quean* wench 26 *pudding*
sausage *his* its 33 *neither* not at all

Countess. To be young again, if we could! I will be a fool
in question, hoping to be the wiser by your answer. I
pray you, sir, are you a courtier?

Lavatch. O Lord, sir! – There's a simple putting off. More, 40
more, a hundred of them.

Countess. Sir, I am a poor friend of yours, that loves you.

Lavatch. O Lord, sir! – Thick, thick, spare not me.

Countess. I think, sir, you can eat none of this homely meat.

Lavatch. O Lord, sir! – Nay, put me to't, I warrant you. 45

Countess. You were lately whipped, sir, as I think.

Lavatch. O Lord, sir! – Spare not me.

Countess. Do you cry, 'O Lord, sir!' at your whipping,
and 'Spare not me'? Indeed, your 'O Lord, sir!' is very
sequent to your whipping; you would answer very well 50
to a whipping, if you were but bound to't.

Lavatch. I ne'er had worse luck in my life in my 'O Lord,
sir!' I see things may serve long, but not serve ever.

Countess. I play the noble housewife with the time,
To entertain it so merrily with a fool. 55

Lavatch. O Lord, sir! – Why, there't serves well again.

Countess. An end, sir! To your business: give Helen this,
And urge her to a present answer back.
Commend me to my kinsmen and my son.
This is not much. 60

Lavatch. Not much commendation to them?

Countess. Not much employment for you. You understand
me?

Lavatch. Most fruitfully. I am there before my legs.

Countess. Haste you again. *Exeunt.* 65

40 *simple putting off* rapid disposal of the question 43 *Thick* quick
49–50 *is . . . to* follows closely upon 50–51 *answer to* repay (with pun
on 'reply') 51 *bound* engaged (with pun on 'tied up') 58 *present* immediate 64 *fruitfully* abundantly 65 *again* back again

     Enter Count [Bertram], Lafew, and Parolles.

Lafew. They say miracles are past, and we have our philosophical persons, to make modern and familiar, things supernatural and causeless. Hence is it that we make trifles of terrors, ensconcing ourselves into seeming
5   knowledge when we should submit ourselves to an unknown fear.

Parolles. Why, 'tis the rarest argument of wonder that hath shot out in our latter times.

Bertram. And so 'tis.

10   *Lafew.* To be relinquished of the artists —

Parolles. So I say — both of Galen and Paracelsus —

Lafew. Of all the learned and authentic fellows —

Parolles. Right! So I say.

Lafew. That gave him out incurable —

15   *Parolles.* Why, there 'tis! so say I too.

Lafew. Not to be helped —

Parolles. Right! as 'twere a man assured of a —

Lafew. Uncertain life, and sure death.

Parolles. Just! you say well. So would I have said.

20   *Lafew.* I may truly say it is a novelty to the world.

Parolles. It is indeed. If you will have it in showing, you shall read it in What-do-ye-call there.

Lafew. [*reads*] 'A showing of a heavenly effect in an earthly actor.'

25   *Parolles.* That's it I would have said, the very same.

II, iii, 2 *modern* commonplace   3 *causeless* of unknown cause   4–5 *ensconcing . . . knowledge* barricading ourselves behind apparent knowledge   5–6 *unknown fear* fear of the unknown   7 *argument* theme   10 *relinquished . . . artists* abandoned by the learned physicians   11 *both . . . Paracelsus* of both schools of medical opinion   12 *authentic fellows* accredited physicians   21 *in showing* visibly, in print   23–24 *A . . . actor* (Lafew evidently reads from a printed ballad celebrating the king's recovery)

Lafew. Why, your dolphin is not lustier. Fore me, I speak
   in respect —

Parolles. Nay, 'tis strange, 'tis very strange! that is the
   brief and the tedious of it; and he's of a most facinerious
   spirit that will not acknowledge it to be the —   30

Lafew. Very hand of heaven —

Parolles. Ay, so I say.

Lafew. In a most weak —

Parolles. And debile minister; great power, great transcend-
   ence, which should indeed give us a further use to be   35
   made than alone the recovery of the king, as to be —

Lafew. Generally thankful.

Enter King, Helena, and Attendants.

Parolles. I would have said it! you say well. Here comes
   the king.

Lafew. Lustick! as the Dutchman says. I'll like a maid the   40
   better whilst I have a tooth in my head. Why, he's able
   to lead her a coranto.

Parolles. Mort du vinaigre! Is not this Helen?

Lafew. Fore God, I think so.

King. Go, call before me all the lords in court.   45
                                        [Exit an Attendant.]
   Sit, my preserver, by thy patient's side,
   And with this healthful hand whose banished sense
   Thou hast repealed, a second time receive
   The confirmation of my promised gift,
   Which but attends thy naming.   50

---

26 *dolphin* (proverbially sportive)   29 *tedious* long   *facinerious* wicked
34 *debile* feeble   40 *Lustick* lusty   42 *coranto* lively dance   43 *Mort du
vinaigre* (expletive of obscure meaning)   48 *repealed* called back   50 *attends* awaits

Enter three or four Lords.

Fair maid, send forth thine eye. This youthful parcel
Of noble bachelors stand at my bestowing,
O'er whom both sovereign power and father's voice
I have to use. Thy frank election make.
55   Thou hast power to choose, and they none to forsake.
    Helena. To each of you one fair and virtuous mistress
    Fall, when Love please; marry, to each but one.
    Lafew. [aside] I'd give bay Curtal and his furniture
    My mouth no more were broken than these boys',
    And writ as little beard.
60 *King.*   Peruse them well:
    Not one of those but had a noble father.
    Helena. Gentlemen,
    Heaven hath through me restored the king to health.
    All. We understand it, and thank heaven for you.
65 *Helena.* I am a simple maid, and therein wealthiest
    That I protest I simply am a maid.
    Please it your majesty, I have done already.
    The blushes in my cheeks thus whisper me,
    'We blush that thou shouldst choose; but be refused,
70   Let the white death sit on thy cheek forever,
    We'll ne'er come there again.'
    King.   Make choice and see;
    Who shuns thy love shuns all his love in me.
    Helena. Now, Dian, from thy altar do I fly,
    And to imperial Love, that god most high,
    Do my sighs stream.   *She addresses her to a Lord.*
75   Sir, will you hear my suit?

---

51 *parcel* group   54 *frank election* unhindered choice   58 *bay Curtal* bay
horse with docked tail   *furniture* trappings   59 *My . . . boys* I still had
all my teeth   60 *writ* claimed   *Peruse* survey

1. Lord. And grant it.

Helena.   Thanks, sir, all the rest is mute.

Lafew. [aside] I had rather be in this choice than throw
    ames-ace for my life.

Helena. [to another] The honor, sir, that flames in your fair
    eyes,

Before I speak, too threat'ningly replies.   80

Love make your fortunes twenty times above

Her that so wishes, and her humble love!

2. Lord. No better, if you please.

Helena.   My wish receive,

Which great Love grant; and so I take my leave.

Lafew. [aside] Do all they deny her? An they were sons of 85
    mine, I'd have them whipped, or I would send them to
    th' Turk to make eunuchs of.

Helena. [to a third] Be not afraid that I your hand should
    take;

I'll never do you wrong for your own sake.

Blessing upon your vows, and in your bed   90

Find fairer fortune, if you ever wed.

Lafew. [aside] These boys are boys of ice; they'll none
    have her. Sure they are bastards to the English; the
    French ne'er got 'em.

Helena. [to a fourth] You are too young, too happy, and
    too good,   95

To make yourself a son out of my blood.

4. Lord. Fair one, I think not so.

Lafew. [aside] There's one grape yet; I am sure thy father
    drunk wine. But if thou be'st not an ass, I am a youth of

78 *ames-ace* a pair of aces, in a cast of dice   83 *No better* i.e. no better
fortune than to be chosen by you   *My wish receive* i.e. my wish, but not
my love   85 *An if*   98 *one grape* one scion of good stock   98–99 *thy . . .
wine* i.e. good blood flows in your veins

100   fourteen; I have known thee already.
        Helena. *[to Bertram]* I dare not say I take you, but I give
            Me and my service, ever whilst I live,
            Into your guiding power. — This is the man.
        King. Why then, young Bertram, take her; she's thy wife.
105 *Bertram.* My wife, my liege? I shall beseech your highness,
            In such a business give me leave to use
            The help of mine own eyes.
        King.   Know'st thou not, Bertram,
            What she has done for me?
        Bertram.   Yes, my good lord;
            But never hope to know why I should marry her.
110 *King.* Thou know'st she has raised me from my sickly bed.
        Bertram. But follows it, my lord, to bring me down
            Must answer for your raising? I know her well;
            She had her breeding at my father's charge.
            A poor physician's daughter my wife? Disdain
115   Rather corrupt me ever!
        King. 'Tis only title thou disdain'st in her, the which
            I can build up. Strange is it that our bloods,
            Of color, weight, and heat, poured all together,
            Would quite confound distinction, yet stands off
120   In differences so mighty. If she be
            All that is virtuous — save what thou dislik'st,
            A poor physician's daughter — thou dislik'st
            Of virtue for the name. But do not so.
            From lowest place when virtuous things proceed,
125   The place is dignified by th' doer's deed.
            Where great additions swell 's, and virtue none,

100 *known* seen through 115 *corrupt me ever* spoil my credit with you for
the rest of my life 118 *Of* in respect to 119 *confound distinction* merge
indistinguishably 119–20 *stands ... mighty* hold aloof as though totally
different 126 *great additions swell 's* solemn titles puff us up

It is a dropsied honor. Good alone
Is good without a name; vileness is so:
The property by what it is should go,
Not by the title. She is young, wise, fair;   130
In these to nature she's immediate heir;
And these breed honor. That is honor's scorn
Which challenges itself as honor's born
And is not like the sire. Honors thrive
When rather from our acts we them derive   135
Than our foregoers. The mere word 's a slave,
Deboshed on every tomb, on every grave
A lying trophy, and as oft is dumb,
Where dust and damned oblivion is the tomb
Of honored bones indeed. What should be said?   140
If thou canst like this creature as a maid,
I can create the rest. Virtue and she
Is her own dower; honor and wealth from me.

Bertram. I cannot love her, nor will strive to do't.

King. Thou wrong'st thyself if thou shouldst strive to
     choose.   145

Helena. That you are well restored, my lord, I'm glad.
Let the rest go.

King. My honor 's at the stake, which to defeat,
I must produce my power. Here, take her hand,
Proud scornful boy, unworthy this good gift,   150
That dost in vile misprision shackle up
My love and her desert; that canst not dream,

---

127 *dropsied* unhealthily swollen 129 *property* quality 131 *immediate*
direct 133–34 *challenges ... sire* claims descent from honorable stock
but does not resemble it 135 *derive* inherit 137 *Deboshed* debauched,
debased 138 *dumb* silent 145 *strive to choose* attempt to choose for
yourself 148 *at the stake* (like a bear being baited) *which* which chal-
lenge 151 *misprision* contempt (with pun on 'false imprisonment')
shackle up i.e. paralyze, render useless

We, poising us in her defective scale,
Shall weigh thee to the beam; that wilt not know,
155   It is in us to plant thine honor where
We please to have it grow. Check thy contempt.
Obey our will, which travails in thy good.
Believe not thy disdain, but presently
Do thine own fortunes that obedient right
160   Which both thy duty owes and our power claims;
Or I will throw thee from my care forever,
Into the staggers and the careless lapse
Of youth and ignorance; both my revenge and hate
Loosing upon thee, in the name of justice,
165   Without all terms of pity. Speak! thine answer!

Bertram. Pardon, my gracious lord; for I submit
My fancy to your eyes. When I consider
What great creation and what dole of honor
Flies where you bid it, I find that she, which late
170   Was in my nobler thoughts most base, is now
The praisèd of the king; who, so ennobled,
Is as 'twere born so.

King.   Take her by the hand,
And tell her she is thine; to whom I promise
A counterpoise, if not to thy estate
A balance more replete.

175 *Bertram.*   I take her hand.

King. Good fortune and the favor of the king

153–54 *poising . . . beam* weighing our royal self on her side of the balance, will outweigh your side and make it touch the crossbar   157 *travails* labors   158 *presently* instantly   159 *obedient right* right of obedience   162 *lapse* fall   165 *Without . . . pity* without pity in any form   168 *dole* share   174–75 *A counterpoise . . . replete* a counterweight (of wealth, by way of dowry), if not an amount great enough to exceed your own estate

Smile upon this contract, whose ceremony
Shall seem expedient on the now-born brief,
And be performed to-night. The solemn feast
Shall more attend upon the coming space, 180
Expecting absent friends. As thou lov'st her,
Thy love's to me religious; else, does err.

Exeunt. Parolles and Lafew stay behind,
commenting of this wedding.

Lafew. Do you hear, monsieur? A word with you.

Parolles. Your pleasure, sir?

Lafew. Your lord and master did well to make his recan- 185
tation.

Parolles. Recantation? my lord? my master?

Lafew. Ay. Is it not a language I speak?

Parolles. A most harsh one, and not to be understood
without bloody succeeding. My master? 190

Lafew. Are you companion to the Count Rossillion?

Parolles. To any count; to all counts; to what is man.

Lafew. To what is count's man; count's master is of
another style.

Parolles. You are too old, sir. Let it satisfy you, you are 195
too old.

Lafew. I must tell thee, sirrah, I write man, to which title
age cannot bring thee.

Parolles. What I dare too well do, I dare not do.

177–78 *whose . . . brief* the consecration of which fittingly follows without delay on this fresh agreement 180 *more . . . space* be deferred a while
longer 181 *Expecting* while we await 182 *religious* scrupulous
190 *bloody succeeding* bloodshed following 191 *companion* fellow (used
belittlingly) 192 *what is man* any true man 193 *count's man* servant
195 *too old* i.e. for me to thrash 197 *write man* claim manhood 199 *What
. . . not do* what I can do all too easily—beat you—the privilege of your
age forbids me to do

200 *Lafew.* I did think thee, for two ordinaries, to be a pretty
wise fellow; thou didst make tolerable vent of thy travel;
it might pass. Yet the scarfs and the bannerets about thee
did manifoldly dissuade me from believing thee a vessel
of too great a burden. I have now found thee; when I
205 lose thee again, I care not. Yet art thou good for nothing
but taking up, and that thou'rt scarce worth.

Parolles. Hadst thou not the privilege of antiquity upon
thee —

Lafew. Do not plunge thyself too far in anger, lest thou
210 hasten thy trial; which if — Lord have mercy on thee for
a hen! So, my good window of lattice, fare thee well; thy
casement I need not open, for I look through thee. Give
me thy hand.

Parolles. My lord, you give me most egregious indignity.

215 *Lafew.* Ay, with all my heart; and thou art worthy of it.

Parolles. I have not, my lord, deserved it.

Lafew. Yes, good faith, every dram of it, and I will not
bate thee a scruple.

Parolles. Well, I shall be wiser.

220 *Lafew.* Ev'n as soon as thou canst, for thou hast to pull at
a smack o' th' contrary. If ever thou be'st bound in thy
scarf and beaten, thou shall find what it is to be proud of
thy bondage. I have a desire to hold my acquaintance
with thee, or rather my knowledge, that I may say, in
225 the default, 'He is a man I know.'

200 *ordinaries* meals 201 *make tolerable vent of* discourse tolerably upon
202 *scarfs* (commonly worn by soldiers) *bannerets* scarfs, looking
like a ship's pennants 204 *burden* cargo *found* seen through 206 *tak-*
ing up purchasing at a discount, as surplus merchandise 211 *lattice* (the
red-latticed window was the mark of an ale-house) 212 *casement* window
look see 218 *bate* deduct *scruple* tiny part 220–21 *pull ... contrary*
take a swig from the large amount of foolishness in yourself 223 *bond-*
age what binds, i.e. the scarf 224–25 *in the default* when you are weighed
and found wanting

Parolles. My lord, you do me most insupportable vexation.

Lafew. I would it were hell-pains for thy sake, and my
poor doing eternal; for doing I am past, as I will by
thee, in what motion age will give me leave.   *Exit.*

Parolles. Well, thou hast a son shall take this disgrace off 230
me, scurvy, old, filthy, scurvy lord! Well, I must be
patient; there is no fettering of authority. I'll beat him,
by my life, if I can meet him with any convenience, an
he were double and double a lord. I'll have no more pity
of his age than I would have of—I'll beat him, an if I 235
could but meet him again.

Enter Lafew.

Lafew. Sirrah, your lord and master's married; there's news
for you. You have a new mistress.

Parolles. I most unfeignedly beseech your lordship to make
some reservation of your wrongs. He is my good lord; 240
whom I serve above is my master.

Lafew. Who? God?

Parolles. Ay, sir.

Lafew. The devil it is that's thy master. Why dost thou
garter up thy arms o' this fashion? Dost make hose of 245
thy sleeves? Do other servants so? Thou wert best set thy
lower part where thy nose stands. By mine honor, if I
were but two hours younger, I'd beat thee. Methink'st
thou art a general offense, and every man should beat
thee. I think thou wast created for men to breathe 250
themselves upon thee.

Parolles. This is hard and undeserved measure, my lord.

228 *for doing* for activity of any kind, especially sexual   228–29 *by
thee* i.e. pass by thee   229 *in what motion* with what speed   233 *an if*
239–40 *make ... wrongs* place some limits to your insults   249 *general
offense* public nuisance   250 *breathe* exercise

Lafew. Go to, sir. You were beaten in Italy for picking a
    kernel out of a pomegranate. You are a vagabond, and
255   no true traveller. You are more saucy with lords and
    honorable personages than the commission of your birth
    and virtue gives you heraldry. You are not worth an-
    other word, else I'd call you knave. I leave you.   *Exit.*

Enter [Bertram] Count Rossillion.

Parolles. Good, very good! It is so then. Good, very good!
260   Let it be concealed awhile.
Bertram. Undone, and forfeited to cares forever!
Parolles. What's the matter, sweetheart?
Bertram. Although before the solemn priest I have sworn,
    I will not bed her.
265 *Parolles.* What? what, sweetheart?
Bertram. O my Parolles, they have married me!
    I'll to the Tuscan wars, and never bed her.
Parolles. France is a dog-hole, and it no more merits
    The tread of a man's foot. To th' wars!
Bertram. There's letters from my mother. What th' import
270   is,
    I know not yet.
Parolles. Ay, that would be known. To th' wars, my boy,
    to th' wars!
    He wears his honor in a box unseen
    That hugs his kicky-wicky here at home,
275   Spending his manly marrow in her arms,
    Which should sustain the bound and high curvet
    Of Mars's fiery steed. To other regions!
    France is a stable; we that dwell in't jades.
    Therefore to th' war!

253–54 *picking . . . pomegranate* i.e. some petty misdemeanor (?)   257 *her-*
aldry authority, warrant   276 *curvet* leap   278 *jades* nags

Bertram. It shall be so. I'll send her to my house,   280
    Acquaint my mother with my hate to her,
    And wherefore I am fled; write to the king
    That which I durst not speak. His present gift
    Shall furnish me to those Italian fields
    Where noble fellows strike. Wars is no strife   285
    To the dark house and the detested wife.
Parolles. Will this capriccio hold in thee? art sure?
Bertram. Go with me to my chamber, and advise me.
    I'll send her straight away. To-morrow
    I'll to the wars, she to her single sorrow.   290
Parolles. Why, these balls bound; there's noise in it! 'Tis
    hard:
    A young man married is a man that's marred.
    Therefore away, and leave her bravely; go.
    The king has done you wrong; but hush, 'tis so. *Exeunt.*

Enter Helena and [Lavatch, the] Clown.   II, iv

Helena. My mother greets me kindly. Is she well?
Lavatch. She is not well, but yet she has her health; she's
    very merry, but yet she is not well. But thanks be given,
    she's very well and wants nothing i' th' world. But yet
    she is not well.   5
Helena. If she be very well, what does she ail that she's not
    very well?
Lavatch. Truly she's very well indeed, but for two things.
Helena. What two things?

286 *To* in comparison with   *dark house* madhouse   287 *capriccio* whim
291 *balls* tennis balls   II, iv, 2 *not well* (evidently alluding to the proverbial belief that all is well with the dead; see l. 10 below)

10 *Lavatch.* One, that she's not in heaven, whither God send
     her quickly; the other, that she's in earth, from whence
     God send her quickly.

Enter Parolles.

Parolles. Bless you, my fortunate lady!

Helena. I hope, sir, I have your good will to have mine
15   own good fortunes.

Parolles. You had my prayers to lead them on, and to
     keep them on have them still. O, my knave, how does
     my old lady?

Lavatch. So that you had her wrinkles and I her money, I
20   would she did as you say.

Parolles. Why, I say nothing.

Lavatch. Marry, you are the wiser man; for many a man's
     tongue shakes out his master's undoing. To say nothing,
     to do nothing, to know nothing, and to have nothing,
25   is to be a great part of your title, which is within a very
     little of nothing.

Parolles. Away! th'art a knave.

Lavatch. You should have said, sir, 'Before a knave th'art
     a knave'; that's 'Before me th'art a knave.' This had
30   been truth, sir.

Parolles. Go to, thou art a witty fool; I have found thee.

Lavatch. Did you find me in yourself, sir, or were you
     taught to find me? . . . The search, sir, was profitable;
     and much fool may you find in you, even to the world's
35   pleasure and the increase of laughter.

Parolles. A good knave, i' faith, and well fed.

19–20 *I . . . say* (meaning obscure) 25 *be . . . title* be very like you, in
status and possessions 28 *Before* in presence of 29 *Before me* 'upon my
word' (with pun on 'ahead of me') 31 *found thee* found thee out 32 *in
yourself* unaided 34 *much . . . in you* much folly may you find in yourself 36 *well fed* i.e. and ill taught (see II, ii, 3)

Madam, my lord will go away to-night;
A very serious business calls on him.
The great prerogative and rite of love,
Which, as your due, time claims, he does acknowledge; 40
But puts it off to a compelled restraint;
Whose want, and whose delay, is strewed with sweets,
Which they distil now in the curbèd time,
To make the coming hour o'erflow with joy
And pleasure drown the brim.

Helena.   What's his will else? 45

Parolles. That you will take your instant leave o' th' king,
And make this haste as your own good proceeding,
Strength'ned with what apology you think
May make it probable need.

Helena.   What more commands he?

Parolles. That, having this obtained, you presently   50
Attend his further pleasure.

Helena. In everything I wait upon his will.

Parolles. I shall report it so.   *Exit Parolles.*

Helena. I pray you. Come, sirrah.   *Exit [with Lavatch].*

❈

Enter Lafew and Bertram.   II, v

Lafew. But I hope your lordship thinks not him a soldier.

Bertram. Yes, my lord, and of very valiant approof.

Lafew. You have it from his own deliverance.

Bertram. And by other warranted testimony.

---

42 *Whose* (referring to the 'rite of love')   43 *they* i.e. people   *curbèd time* period of distillation   45 *else* besides   49 *probable* plausible   50 *presently* immediately   51 *Attend* await   52 *wait upon* serve   II, v, 2 *very valiant approof* proved valor

5 *Lafew.* Then my dial goes not true; I took this lark for a
     bunting.

Bertram. I do assure you, my lord, he is very great in
     knowledge and accordingly valiant.

Lafew. I have then sinned against his experience and trans-
10   gressed against his valor; and my state that way is dan-
     gerous, since I cannot yet find in my heart to repent.

Enter Parolles.

Here he comes. I pray you make us friends; I will pursue
     the amity.

Parolles. [*to Bertram*] These things shall be done, sir.

15 *Lafew.* Pray you, sir, who's his tailor?

Parolles. Sir?

Lafew. O, I know him well, I, sir. He, sir, 's a good work-
     man, a very good tailor.

Bertram. [*aside to Parolles*] Is she gone to the king?

20 *Parolles.* She is.

Bertram. Will she away to-night?

Parolles. As you'll have her.

Bertram. I have writ my letters, casketed my treasure,
     Given order for our horses; and to-night,
25   When I should take possession of the bride,
     End ere I do begin.

Lafew. A good traveller is something at the latter end of a
     dinner; but one that lies three thirds and uses a known
     truth to pass a thousand nothings with, should be once
30   heard and thrice beaten. God save you, captain.

---

5 *dial* 'the compass of my judgment'   6 *bunting* common field bird   8 *ac-
cordingly* correspondingly   10–11 *my . . . dangerous* my soul is in peril
15 *who's his tailor* i.e. who made this manikin   27–28 *at . . . dinner* i.e.
to relate his travels

Bertram. Is there any unkindness between my lord and you, monsieur?

Parolles. I know not how I have deserved to run into my lord's displeasure.

Lafew. You have made shift to run into't, boots and spurs 35 and all, like him that leapt into the custard; and out of it you'll run again rather than suffer question for your residence.

Bertram. It may be you have mistaken him, my lord.

Lafew. And shall do so ever, though I took him at 's 40 prayers. Fare you well, my lord, and believe this of me: there can be no kernel in this light nut; the soul of this man is his clothes. Trust him not in matter of heavy consequence. I have kept of them tame and know their natures. — Farewell, monsieur. I have spoken better of 45 you than you have or will to deserve at my hand; but we must do good against evil.   [*Exit.*]

Parolles. An idle lord, I swear.

Bertram. I think so.

Parolles. Why, do you not know him?   50

Bertram. Yes, I do know him well, and common speech
Gives him a worthy pass.

Enter Helena.

Here comes my clog.

Helena. I have, sir, as I was commanded from you,
Spoke with the king, and have procured his leave
For present parting; only he desires   55
Some private speech with you.

36 *him ... custard* the clown that jumped into the custard at the yearly Lord Mayor's feast   37–38 *suffer ... residence* explain your presence there   40 *do so* mis-take, put an unfavorable interpretation on   44 *kept ... tame* kept such creatures as household pets   48 *idle* foolish   52 *pass* reputation   55 *present* immediate

Bertram.   I shall obey his will.
   You must not marvel, Helen, at my course,
   Which holds not color with the time, nor does
   The ministration and requirèd office
60 On my particular. Prepared I was not
   For such a business; therefore am I found
   So much unsettled. This drives me to entreat you
   That presently you take your way for home,
   And rather muse than ask why I entreat you;
65 For my respects are better than they seem,
   And my appointments have in them a need
   Greater than shows itself at the first view
   To you that know them not. This to my mother.

                               [Gives a letter.]

   'Twill be two days ere I shall see you; so
   I leave you to your wisdom.
70 *Helena.*   Sir, I can nothing say
   But that I am your most obedient servant.
Bertram. Come, come; no more of that.
Helena.   And ever shall
   With true observance seek to eke out that
   Wherein toward me my homely stars have failed
   To equal my great fortune.
75 *Bertram.*   Let that go;
   My haste is very great. Farewell. Hie home.
Helena. Pray, sir, your pardon.
Bertram.   Well, what would you say?
Helena. I am not worthy of the wealth I owe,
   Nor dare I say 'tis mine; and yet it is —

58 *holds . . . time* seems inappropriate to the occasion   58–60 *nor . . . particular* nor fulfills my obligations as a husband   64 *muse* remain in wonder   65 *respects* reasons 66 *appointments* arrangements 73 *observance* dutiful service *eke out* supplement 74 *homely stars* humble origins 78 *owe* own

But, like a timorous thief, most fain would steal   80
  What law does vouch mine own.
Bertram.   What would you have?
Helena. Something, and scarce so much; nothing, indeed.
  I would not tell you what I would, my lord.
  Faith, yes —
  Strangers and foes do sunder, and not kiss.   85
Bertram. I pray you stay not, but in haste to horse.
Helena. I shall not break your bidding, good my lord.
Bertram. Where are my other men, monsieur? Farewell.
  Go thou toward home —   *Exit [Helena].*
                    where I will never come
  Whilst I can shake my sword or hear the drum.   90
  Away, and for our flight!
Parolles.   Bravely, coragio!   *[Exeunt.]*

Flourish. Enter the Duke of Florence, the two Frenchmen,   III, i
    with a Troop of Soldiers.

Duke. So that from point to point now have you heard
  The fundamental reasons of this war,
  Whose great decision hath much blood let forth,
  And more thirsts after.
1. Lord.   Holy seems the quarrel
  Upon your grace's part; black and fearful   5
  On the opposer.
Duke. Therefore we marvel much our cousin France
  Would in so just a business shut his bosom
  Against our borrowing prayers.
2. Lord.   Good my lord,

80 *fain* gladly 81 *vouch* confirm 91 *coragio* courage III, i, 3 *whose great decision* the deciding of which 7 *cousin* fellow ruler

10 The reasons of our state I cannot yield
But like a common and an outward man
That the great figure of a council frames
By self-unable motion — therefore dare not
Say what I think of it, since I have found
15 Myself in my incertain grounds to fail
As often as I guessed.

Duke.   Be it his pleasure.

1. Lord. But I am sure the younger of our nature,
That surfeit on their ease, will day by day
Come here for physic.

Duke.   Welcome shall they be;
20 And all the honors that can fly from us
Shall on them settle. You know your places well;
When better fall, for your avails they fell.
To-morrow to th' field.   *Flourish. [Exeunt.]*

III, ii   *Enter Countess and [Lavatch, the] Clown.*

Countess. It hath happened all as I would have had it, save
that he comes not along with her.

Lavatch. By my troth, I take my young lord to be a very
melancholy man.

5 *Countess.* By what observance, I pray you?

Lavatch. Why, he will look upon his boot, and sing; mend
the ruff, and sing; ask questions, and sing; pick his teeth,

10 *yield* report   11–13 *a common ... motion* an unskilled outsider who
imperfectly imagines to himself the great deliberations proceeding in
secret   17 *nature* disposition   19 *physic* medicine   22 *When ... fell*
when better places fall vacant, they will become yours   III, ii, 5 *observance*
observation

and sing. I know a man that had this trick of melancholy
sold a goodly manor for a song.

Countess. Let me see what he writes, and when he means   10
to come.   [*Opens a letter.*]

Lavatch. I have no mind to Isbel since I was at court. Our
old lings and our Isbels o' th' country are nothing like
your old ling and your Isbels o' th' court. The brains of
my Cupid 's knocked out, and I begin to love, as an old   15
man loves money, with no stomach.

Countess. What have we here?

Lavatch. E'en that you have there.   *Exit.*

[*Countess reads*] *a letter.* 'I have sent you a daughter-in-
law. She hath recovered the king, and undone me. I have   20
wedded her, not bedded her, and sworn to make the
"not" eternal. You shall hear I am run away; know it
before the report come. If there be breadth enough in the
world, I will hold a long distance. My duty to you.

> Your unfortunate son,   25
> BERTRAM.'

This is not well, rash and unbridled boy,
To fly the favors of so good a king,
To pluck his indignation on thy head
By the misprizing of a maid too virtuous   30
For the contempt of empire.

Enter [Lavatch, the] Clown.

Lavatch. O madam, yonder is heavy news within between two soldiers and my young lady!

Countess. What is the matter?

Lavatch. Nay, there is some comfort in the news, some   35

---

13 *old lings* salted cods 16 *stomach* appetite, inclination 31 *For . . .
empire* for even an emperor to scorn 32 *heavy* sad

comfort—your son will not be killed so soon as I
thought he would.

Countess. Why should he be killed?

Lavatch. So say I, madam, if he run away, as I hear he does.
40 The danger is in standing to't; that's the loss of men,
though it be the getting of children. Here they come will
tell you more. For my part, I only hear your son was run
away.   *[Exit.]*

Enter Helena and [the] two [French] Gentlemen.

2. Lord. Save you, good madam.
45 *Helena.* Madam, my lord is gone, forever gone!
1. Lord. Do not say so.
Countess. Think upon patience. Pray you, gentlemen —
I have felt so many quirks of joy and grief
That the first face of neither on the start
50 Can woman me unto't. Where is my son, I pray you?
1. Lord. Madam, he's gone to serve the Duke of Florence.
We met him thitherward, for thence we came;
And after some dispatch in hand at court,
Thither we bend again.
55 *Helena.* Look on his letter, madam. Here's my passport.
[Reads] 'When thou canst get the ring upon my finger,
which never shall come off, and show me a child begotten
of thy body that I am father to, then call me husband;
but in such a "then" I write a "never."'
60 This is a dreadful sentence.
Countess. Brought you this letter, gentlemen?
1. Lord.   Ay, madam,
And for the contents' sake are sorry for our pains.
Countess. I prithee, lady, have a better cheer.

40 *standing to't* meeting danger head on (with sexual quibble) 41 *getting* be-
getting 48 *quirks* spells 50 *woman me* make me womanish, make me weep

84

If thou engrossest all the griefs are thine,
Thou robb'st me of a moiety. He was my son,   65
But I do wash his name out of my blood,
And thou art all my child. Towards Florence is he?

1. Lord. Ay, madam.

Countess.   And to be a soldier?

1. Lord. Such is his noble purpose, and believe't,
The duke will lay upon him all the honor   70
That good convenience claims.

Countess.   Return you thither?

2. Lord. Ay, madam, with the swiftest wing of speed.

Helena. [reads] 'Till I have no wife, I have nothing in
France.'
'Tis bitter.

Countess. Find you that there?

Helena.   Ay, madam.

2. Lord. 'Tis but the boldness of his hand haply, which his   75
heart was not consenting to.

Countess. Nothing in France until he have no wife!
There's nothing here that is too good for him
But only she, and she deserves a lord
That twenty such rude boys might tend upon   80
And call her hourly mistress. Who was with him?

2. Lord. A servant only, and a gentleman
Which I have sometime known.

Countess.   Parolles, was it not?

2. Lord. Ay, my good lady, he.

Countess. A very tainted fellow, and full of wickedness.   85
My son corrupts a well-derivèd nature

---

64 *engrossest* monopolize *are* which are 65 *moiety* half 67 *all my child*
my only child 71 *convenience* fitness 75 *haply* perhaps 85 *tainted*
depraved 86 *well-derivèd nature* inherited goodness

With his inducement.

2. *Lord.*   Indeed, good lady,
The fellow has a deal of that too much
Which holds him much to have.

Countess.   Y'are welcome, gentlemen.

90   I will entreat you, when you see my son,
To tell him that his sword can never win
The honor that he loses. More I'll entreat you
Written to bear along.

1. *Lord.*   We serve you, madam,
In that and all your worthiest affairs.

95 *Countess.* Not so, but as we change our courtesies.
Will you draw near?   *Exit [with the Gentlemen].*
Helena. 'Till I have no wife I have nothing in France.'
Nothing in France until he has no wife!
Thou shalt have none, Rossillion, none in France;

100   Then hast thou all again. Poor lord, is't I
That chase thee from thy country, and expose
Those tender limbs of thine to the event
Of the none-sparing war? And is it I
That drive thee from the sportive court, where thou

105   Wast shot at with fair eyes, to be the mark
Of smoky muskets? O you leaden messengers
That ride upon the violent speed of fire,
Fly with false aim; move the still-piecing air,
That sings with piercing; do not touch my lord!

110   Whoever shoots at him, I set him there.
Whoever charges on his forward breast,

---

87 *With his inducement* by his (Parolles') ill counsel 88–89 *has . . .
have* possesses far too much of that power to mislead that endears him to
Bertram 93 *Written* in writing 95 *Not so . . . courtesies* you serve me
only in the sense that we mutually serve each other 96 *draw near* come
in 102 *event* outcome 105 *mark* target 108 *still-piecing* always closing again

I am the caitiff that do hold him to't.
And though I kill him not, I am the cause
His death was so effected. Better 'twere
I met the ravin lion when he roared   115
With sharp constraint of hunger; better 'twere
That all the miseries which nature owes
Were mine at once. No; come thou home, Rossillion,
Whence honor but of danger wins a scar,
As oft it loses all. I will be gone.   120
My being here it is that holds thee hence.
Shall I stay here to do't? No, no, although
The air of paradise did fan the house
And angels officed all. I will be gone,
That pitiful rumor may report my flight   125
To consolate thine ear. Come, night; end, day;
For with the dark poor thief I'll steal away.   *Exit.*

Flourish. Enter the Duke of Florence, [Bertram Count]   III, iii
Rossillion, Drum and Trumpets, Soldiers, Parolles.

Duke. The general of our horse thou art; and we,
  Great in our hope, lay our best love and credence
  Upon thy promising fortune.
Bertram.   Sir, it is
  A charge too heavy for my strength, but yet
  We'll strive to bear it for your worthy sake   5
  To th' extreme edge of hazard.

112 *caitiff* wretch 115 *ravin* ravenous 117 *owes* owns 119–20 *Whence
... all* from where honor wins nothing from danger but scars, and sometimes pays with its life 124 *officed all* did all the household chores 125 *pitiful* i.e. full of pity for Bertram 126 *consolate* console III, iii, 2 *Great*
pregnant 6 *edge of hazard* limit of danger

Duke.   Then go thou forth,
And Fortune play upon thy prosperous helm
As thy auspicious mistress!
Bertram.   This very day,
Great Mars, I put myself into thy file.
10   Make me but like my thoughts, and I shall prove
A lover of thy drum, hater of love.   *Exeunt omnes.*

III, iv   *Enter Countess and Steward.*

Countess. Alas! and would you take the letter of her?
Might you not know she would do as she has done,
By sending me a letter? Read it again.
[Steward reads the] letter.
'I am Saint Jaques' pilgrim, thither gone.
5   Ambitious love hath so in me offended
That barefoot plod I the cold ground upon,
     With sainted vow my faults to have amended.
Write, write, that from the bloody course of war
My dearest master, your dear son, may hie.
10 Bless him at home in peace, whilst I from far
     His name with zealous fervor sanctify.
His taken labors bid him me forgive.
     I, his despiteful Juno, sent him forth
From courtly friends, with camping foes to live,
15   Where death and danger dogs the heels of worth.
He is too good and fair for death and me;
     Whom I myself embrace to set him free.'
Countess. Ah, what sharp stings are in her mildest words!

9 *file* ranks   10 *like my thoughts* i.e. valiant   III, iv, 4 *thither* i.e. to the shrine of Saint Jaques, at Compostella   12 *taken* undertaken   13 *despiteful* cruel   17 *Whom* death   *him* Bertram

Rinaldo, you did never lack advice so much
As letting her pass so. Had I spoke with her,   20
I could have well diverted her intents,
Which thus she hath prevented.
Steward.   Pardon me, madam.
If I had given you this at overnight,
She might have been o'erta'en; and yet she writes
Pursuit would be but vain.
Countess.   What angel shall   25
Bless this unworthy husband? He cannot thrive,
Unless her prayers, whom heaven delights to hear
And loves to grant, reprieve him from the wrath
Of greatest justice. Write, write, Rinaldo,
To this unworthy husband of his wife.   30
Let every word weigh heavy of her worth
That he does weigh too light. My greatest grief,
Though little he do feel it, set down sharply.
Dispatch the most convenient messenger.
When haply he shall hear that she is gone,   35
He will return; and hope I may that she,
Hearing so much, will speed her foot again,
Led hither by pure love. Which of them both
Is dearest to me, I have no skill in sense
To make distinction. Provide this messenger.   40
My heart is heavy, and mine age is weak.
Grief would have tears, and sorrow bids me speak.
                                              Exeunt.

19 *advice* judgment   22 *prevented* forestalled   23 *at overnight* last night
32 *weigh* value   35 *haply* perchance   39 *skill* ability   *sense* feeling

III, v   *A tucket afar off. Enter old Widow of Florence, her*
         Daughter [Diana], Violenta, and Mariana, with other
         Citizens.

Widow. Nay, come; for if they do approach the city, we
shall lose all the sight.

Diana. They say the French count has done most honorable service.

5 *Widow.* It is reported that he has taken their great'st com-
mander, and that with his own hand he slew the duke's
brother. [*Tucket.*] We have lost our labor; they are gone
a contrary way. Hark! You may know by their trumpets.

Mariana. Come, let's return again, and suffice ourselves
10 with the report of it. Well, Diana, take heed of this
French earl. The honor of a maid is her name, and no
legacy is so rich as honesty.

Widow. I have told my neighbor how you have been
solicited by a gentleman his companion.

15 *Mariana.* I know that knave, hang him! one Parolles, a
filthy officer he is in those suggestions for the young earl.
Beware of them, Diana; their promises, enticements,
oaths, tokens, and all these engines of lust, are not the
things they go under. Many a maid hath been seduced
20 by them; and the misery is, example, that so terrible
shows in the wrack of maidenhood, cannot for all that
dissuade succession but that they are limed with the
twigs that threatens them. I hope I need not to advise
you further, but I hope your own grace will keep you

III, v S.D. *tucket* trumpet fanfare   9 *suffice* satisfy   12 *honesty* chastity
16 *officer* agent   *suggestions* enticements   18 *engines* artifices   19 *go under*
pretend to be   20 *example* past precedent   20–21 *so . . . maidenhood* is so
filled with terrifying instances of wrecked maidenhoods   22 *dissuade succession* discourage others from following the same course   *they* i.e. other
maidens   22–23 *limed . . . twigs* caught in the snares

where you are, though there were no further danger 25
known but the modesty which is so lost.

Diana. You shall not need to fear me.

Enter Helena, [like a pilgrim].

Widow. I hope so. Look, here comes a pilgrim. I know she
will lie at my house; thither they send one another. I'll
question her.   30

God save you, pilgrim! Whither are you bound?

Helena. To Saint Jaques le Grand.

Where do the palmers lodge, I do beseech you?

Widow. At the Saint Francis here, beside the port.

Helena. Is this the way?   35

Widow. Ay, marry, is't.   *A march afar.*

Hark you! they come this way.

If you will tarry, holy pilgrim,

But till the troops come by,

I will conduct you where you shall be lodged,

The rather for I think I know your hostess   40

As ample as myself.

Helena.   Is it yourself?

Widow. If you shall please so, pilgrim.

Helena. I thank you, and will stay upon your leisure.

Widow. You came, I think, from France?

Helena.   I did so.

Widow. Here you shall see a countryman of yours   45

That has done worthy service.

Helena.   His name, I pray you?

Diana. The Count Rossillion. Know you such a one?

Helena. But by the ear, that hears most nobly of him;

---

25 *further danger* i.e. pregnancy 27 *fear* mistrust 29 *lie* lodge 34 *the
Saint Francis* (an inn) *port* city gate 36 *marry* indeed 41 *ample* well
43 *stay upon* await

His face I know not.

Diana.   Whatsome'er he is,
50 He's bravely taken here. He stole from France,
    As 'tis reported, for the king had married him
    Against his liking. Think you it is so?

Helena. Ay, surely, mere the truth; I know his lady.

Diana. There is a gentleman that serves the count
    Reports but coarsely of her.

55 *Helena.*   What's his name?

Diana. Monsieur Parolles.

Helena.   O, I believe with him,
    In argument of praise or to the worth
    Of the great count himself, she is too mean
    To have her name repeated. All her deserving
60 Is a reservèd honesty, and that
    I have not heard examined.

Diana.   Alas, poor lady!
    'Tis a hard bondage to become the wife
    Of a detesting lord.

Widow. I write, good creature, wheresoe'er she is,
    Her heart weighs sadly. This young maid might
65   do her
    A shrewd turn, if she pleased.

Helena.   How do you mean?
    May be the amorous count solicits her
    In the unlawful purpose.

Widow.   He does indeed,
    And brokes with all that can in such a suit

---

50 *bravely taken* made a splendid impression   53 *mere the truth* the absolute truth   57 *In . . . praise* if it comes to praising her   *to* compared
to   59 *All her deserving* her only merit   60 *reservèd honesty* preserved
chastity   61 *examined* called into question   64 *write* certify, declare
66 *shrewd* ill-natured   69 *brokes* bargains

Corrupt the tender honor of a maid;   70
But she is armed for him, and keeps her guard
In honestest defense.

Drum and Colors. Enter [Bertram] Count Rossillion, Pa-
rolles, and the whole Army.

Mariana.   The gods forbid else!
Widow. So, now they come.
  That is Antonio, the duke's eldest son;
  That, Escalus.
Helena.   Which is the Frenchman?
Diana.   He —   75
  That with the plume. 'Tis a most gallant fellow;
  I would he loved his wife. If he were honester,
  He were much goodlier. Is't not a handsome gentleman?
Helena. I like him well.
Diana. 'Tis pity he is not honest. Yond's that same knave   80
  That leads him to these places. Were I his lady,
  I would poison that vile rascal.
Helena.   Which is he?
Diana. That jackanapes with scarfs. Why is he melancholy?
Helena. Perchance he's hurt i' th' battle.
Parolles. Lose our drum? Well!   85
Mariana. He's shrewdly vexed at something. Look, he has
    spied us.
Widow. Marry, hang you!
Mariana. And your curtsy, for a ring-carrier!
                    Exeunt [Bertram, Parolles, and Army].
Widow. The troop is past. Come, pilgrim, I will bring you
  Where you shall host. Of enjoined penitents   90

77 *honester* more honorable   81 *places* infamous actions (?)   86 *shrewdly*
sorely   88 *curtsy* ceremony *ring-carrier* go-between   90 *host* lodge *enjoined*
penitents pilgrims bound by oath to their pilgrimage

There's four or five, to great Saint Jaques bound,
Already at my house.
Helena.   I humbly thank you.
Please it this matron and this gentle maid
To eat with us to-night, the charge and thanking
95   Shall be for me; and, to requite you further,
I will bestow some precepts of this virgin,
Worthy the note.
Both.   We'll take your offer kindly.   *Exeunt.*

III, vi   *Enter [Bertram] Count Rossillion and the Frenchmen, as*
        at first.

2. *Lord.* Nay, good my lord, put him to't; let him have
his way.
1. *Lord.* If your lordship find him not a hilding, hold me
no more in your respect.
5 2. *Lord.* On my life, my lord, a bubble.
Bertram. Do you think I am so far deceived in him?
2. *Lord.* Believe it, my lord, in mine own direct knowledge,
without any malice, but to speak of him as my kinsman,
he's a most notable coward, an infinite and endless liar,
10   an hourly promise-breaker, the owner of no one good
quality worthy your lordship's entertainment.
1. *Lord.* It were fit you knew him, lest reposing too far in
his virtue, which he hath not, he might at some great
and trusty business in a main danger fail you.

---

94 *charge and thanking* both expense and gratitude   96 *of* on   III, vi, 3 *hild-*
ing base fellow   5 *bubble* impostor   8 *as* as if he were   11 *entertain-*
ment maintenance

Bertram. I would I knew in what particular action to try 15
him.

1. Lord. None better than to let him fetch off his drum,
which you hear him so confidently undertake to do.

2. Lord. I with a troop of Florentines will suddenly surprise
him; such I will have whom I am sure he knows not 20
from the enemy. We will bind and hoodwink him so,
that he shall suppose no other but that he is carried into
the leaguer of the adversaries when we bring him to our
own tents. Be but your lordship present at his examina-
tion. If he do not, for the promise of his life and in the 25
highest compulsion of base fear, offer to betray you and
deliver all the intelligence in his power against you, and
that with the divine forfeit of his soul upon oath, never
trust my judgment in anything.

1. Lord. O, for the love of laughter, let him fetch his drum! 30
He says he has a stratagem for't. When your lordship
sees the bottom of his success in't, and to what metal
this counterfeit lump of ore will be melted, if you give
him not John Drum's entertainment, your inclining cannot be removed. Here he comes.   35

Enter Parolles.

2. Lord. O, for the love of laughter, hinder not the honor
of his design; let him fetch off his drum in any hand.

Bertram. How now, monsieur? This drum sticks sorely in
your disposition.

1. Lord. A pox on't, let it go! 'tis but a drum.   40

Parolles. But a drum? Is't but a drum? A drum so lost!
There was excellent command: to charge in with our

21 *hoodwink* blindfold 23 *leaguer* camp 32 *bottom* extent 34 *John
Drum's entertainment* unceremonious dismissal *inclining* partiality 37 *in
any hand* in any case

horse upon our own wings and to rend our own soldiers!

1. *Lord.* That was not to be blamed in the command of
45   the service; it was a disaster of war that Caesar himself
could not have prevented if he had been there to
command.

Bertram. Well, we cannot greatly condemn our success.
Some dishonor we had in the loss of that drum, but it
50   is not to be recovered.

Parolles. It might have been recovered.

Bertram. It might, but it is not now.

Parolles. It is to be recovered. But that the merit of service
is seldom attributed to the true and exact performer, I
55   would have that drum or another, or *hic jacet*!

Bertram. Why, if you have a stomach, to't, monsieur! If
you think your mystery in stratagem can bring this
instrument of honor again into his native quarter, be
magnanimous in the enterprise and go on; I will grace
60   the attempt for a worthy exploit. If you speed well in
it, the duke shall both speak of it and extend to you what
further becomes his greatness, even to the utmost syllable
of your worthiness.

Parolles. By the hand of a soldier, I will undertake it.

65 *Bertram.* But you must not now slumber in it.

Parolles. I'll about it this evening, and I will presently pen
down my dilemmas, encourage myself in my certainty,
put myself into my mortal preparation; and by midnight look to hear further from me.

70 *Bertram.* May I be bold to acquaint his grace you are gone
about it?

48 *success* fortune   55 *hic jacet* 'here lies'; i.e. 'or die in the attempt'
57 *mystery* skill   58 *again . . . quarter* back home   59 *grace* honor
60 *speed* succeed   66 *presently* immediately   67 *dilemmas* arguments (?)
68 *mortal* death-dealing

Parolles. I know not what the success will be, my lord, but the attempt I vow.

Bertram. I know th'art valiant, and to the possibility of thy soldiership will subscribe for thee. Farewell.   75

Parolles. I love not many words.   *Exit.*

2. Lord. No more than a fish loves water. Is not this a strange fellow, my lord, that so confidently seems to undertake this business, which he knows is not to be done; damns himself to do, and dares better be damned 80 than to do't?

1. Lord. You do not know him, my lord, as we do. Certain it is that he will steal himself into a man's favor, and for a week escape a great deal of discoveries; but when you find him out, you have him ever after.   85

Bertram. Why, do you think he will make no deed at all of this that so seriously he does address himself unto?

2. Lord. None in the world; but return with an invention, and clap upon you two or three probable lies. But we have almost embossed him. You shall see his fall to-night; 90 for indeed he is not for your lordship's respect.

1. Lord. We'll make you some sport with the fox ere we case him. He was first smoked by the old Lord Lafew. When his disguise and he is parted, tell me what a sprat you shall find him, which you shall see this very night. 95

2. Lord. I must go look my twigs; he shall be caught.

Bertram. Your brother, he shall go along with me.

2. Lord. As't please your lordship. I'll leave you.   *[Exit.]*

Bertram. Now will I lead you to the house, and show you
    The lass I spoke of.

---

74 *possibility* capacity   75 *subscribe for* answer for   85 *have him* have his number   89 *probable* plausible   90 *embossed* driven to extremity 93 *case* uncase, unmask   *smoked* smoked out   94 *sprat* contemptible creature   96 *look my twigs* look after my traps

100   *1. Lord.*   But you say she's honest.
       Bertram. That's all the fault. I spoke with her but once
          And found her wondrous cold, but I sent to her,
          By this same coxcomb that we have i' th' wind,
          Tokens and letters, which she did resend,
105   And this is all I have done. She's a fair creature;
          Will you go see her?
       1. Lord.   With all my heart, my lord.
                                   Exeunt.

III, vii   *Enter Helena and Widow.*

   Helena. If you misdoubt me that I am not she,
         I know not how I shall assure you further
         But I shall lose the grounds I work upon.
   Widow. Though my estate be fallen, I was well born,
5   Nothing acquainted with these businesses,
         And would not put my reputation now
         In any staining act.
   Helena.   Nor would I wish you.
         First give me trust the count he is my husband,
         And what to your sworn counsel I have spoken
10   Is so from word to word; and then you cannot,
         By the good aid that I of you shall borrow,
         Err in bestowing it.
   Widow.   I should believe you,
         For you have showed me that which well approves

---

100 *honest* chaste   103 *coxcomb* fool   *that ... wind* whom we're hunting
104 *resend* send back   III, vii, 1 *misdoubt* doubt   3 *But ... upon* unless I
wreck my plans by disclosing my identity to Bertram   4 *estate* condition
10 *from ... word* in every particular   11 *By* in respect to

Y'are great in fortune.
Helena.   Take this purse of gold,
And let me buy your friendly help thus far,   15
Which I will overpay, and pay again
When I have found it. The count he woos your daughter,
Lays down his wanton siege before her beauty,
Resolved to carry her. Let her in fine consent,
As we'll direct her how 'tis best to bear it.   20
Now his important blood will naught deny
That she'll demand. A ring the county wears
That downward hath succeeded in his house
From son to son some four or five descents
Since the first father wore it. This ring he holds   25
In most rich choice; yet in his idle fire,
To buy his will, it would not seem too dear,
Howe'er repented after.
Widow.   Now I see
The bottom of your purpose.
Helena. You see it lawful then; it is no more   30
But that your daughter, ere she seems as won,
Desires this ring; appoints him an encounter;
In fine, delivers me to fill the time,
Herself most chastely absent. After,
To marry her, I'll add three thousand crowns   35
To what is passed already.
Widow.   I have yielded.
Instruct my daughter how she shall persever,
That time and place with this deceit so lawful
May prove coherent. Every night he comes
With musics of all sorts, and songs composed   40

19 *in fine* at length   21 *important* importunate   22 *county* count   26 *most rich choice* highest esteem   *idle* careless   27 *will* pleasure   39 *coherent* in accord

99

To her unworthiness. It nothing steads us
To chide him from our eaves, for he persists
As if his life lay on't.

Helena. Why then to-night
Let us assay our plot, which if it speed,
45 Is wicked meaning in a lawful deed,
And lawful meaning in a lawful act,
Where both not sin, and yet a sinful fact.
But let's about it. [*Exeunt.*]

IV, i *Enter one of the Frenchmen, [the Second Lord,] with five*
or six other Soldiers, in ambush.

2. Lord. He can come no other way but by this hedge
corner. When you sally upon him, speak what terrible
language you will; though you understand it not yourselves, no matter; for we must not seem to understand
5 him, unless some one among us whom we must produce
for an interpreter.

1. Soldier. Good captain, let me be th' interpreter.

2. Lord. Art not acquainted with him? Knows he not thy
voice?

10 *1. Soldier.* No, sir, I warrant you.

2. Lord. But what linsey-woolsey hast thou to speak to us
again?

1. Soldier. E'en such as you speak to me.

2. Lord. He must think us some band of strangers i' th'
15 adversary's entertainment. Now he hath a smack of all

41 *steads* avails 44 *speed* succeed 45 *meaning* intention 47 *fact* deed,
crime IV, i, 5 *unless* except for 11 *linsey-woolsey* gibberish 14 *strangers*
foreigners 15 *entertainment* employment

neighboring languages; therefore we must every one be
a man of his own fancy, not to know what we speak
one to another; so we seem to know, is to know straight
our purpose. Choughs' language – gabble enough, and
good enough. As for you, interpreter, you must seem   20
very politic. But couch, ho! Here he comes, to beguile
two hours in a sleep, and then to return and swear the
lies he forges.   [*They hide.*]

Enter Parolles.

Parolles. Ten o'clock. Within these three hours 'twill be
time enough to go home. What shall I say I have done?   25
It must be a very plausive invention that carries it. They
begin to smoke me, and disgraces have of late knocked
too often at my door. I find my tongue is too foolhardy;
but my heart hath the fear of Mars before it, and of his
creatures, not daring the reports of my tongue.   30
2. Lord. This is the first truth that e'er thine own tongue
was guilty of.
Parolles. What the devil should move me to undertake the
recovery of this drum, being not ignorant of the impossibility, and knowing I had no such purpose? I must   35
give myself some hurts and say I got them in exploit;
yet slight ones will not carry it. They will say, 'Came
you off with so little?' And great ones I dare not give.
Wherefore, what's the instance? Tongue, I must put
you into a butter-woman's mouth, and buy myself an-   40

17 *of . . . fancy* with a fancied language of his own   18–19 *so . . . purpose*
it will suffice if we merely seem to understand each other   19 *Choughs'*
jackdaws'   21 *politic* cunning   *couch, ho* to our hiding-places   26 *plausive*
plausible   27 *smoke* detect   29–30 *his   creatures* soldiers   30 *not . . .
tongue* not daring to imitate my tongue's audacity   39 *instance* evidence (?)
40 *butter-woman* (a proverbial scold)

other of Bajazet's mule, if you prattle me into these perils.

2. Lord. Is it possible he should know what he is, and be
that he is?

Parolles. I would the cutting of my garments would serve
45   the turn, or the breaking of my Spanish sword.

2. Lord. We cannot afford you so.

Parolles. Or the baring of my beard, and to say it was in
stratagem.

2. Lord. 'Twould not do.

50   *Parolles.* Or to drown my clothes, and say I was stripped.

2. Lord. Hardly serve.

Parolles. Though I swore I leapt from the window of the
citadel —

2. Lord. How deep?

55   *Parolles.* Thirty fathom.

2. Lord. Three great oaths would scarce make that be
believed.

Parolles. I would I had any drum of the enemy's; I would
swear I recovered it.

60   *2. Lord.* You shall hear one anon.

Parolles. A drum now of the enemy's —   *Alarum within.*

2. Lord. Throca movousus, cargo, cargo, cargo.

All. Cargo, cargo, cargo, villianda par corbo, cargo.

Parolles. O, ransom, ransom! Do not hide mine eyes.
                                        [They blindfold him.]

65   *[1. Soldier as] Interpreter.* Boskos thromuldo boskos.

Parolles. I know you are the Muskos' regiment,
And I shall lose my life for want of language.
If there be here German, or Dane, Low Dutch,
Italian, or French, let him speak to me,

---

41 *Bajazet's mule* (unexplained)   46 *afford you so* let you off so easily
47 *baring* shaving   67 *want of language* ignorance of your language

I'll discover that which shall undo the Florentine.   70

Interpreter. Boskos vauvado. I understand thee, and can
    speak thy tongue. Kerelybonto. Sir, betake thee to thy
    faith, for seventeen poniards are at thy bosom.

Parolles. O!

Interpreter. O, pray, pray, pray! Manka revania dulche.   75

2. Lord. Oscorbidulchos volivorco.

Interpreter. The general is content to spare thee yet,
    And, hoodwinked as thou art, will lead thee on
    To gather from thee. Haply thou mayst inform
    Something to save thy life.

Parolles.   O, let me live,   80
    And all the secrets of our camp I'll show,
    Their force, their purposes; nay, I'll speak that
    Which you will wonder at.

Interpreter.   But wilt thou faithfully?

Parolles. If I do not, damn me.

Interpreter. Acordo linta. Come on; thou art granted space.   85
            Exit [with Parolles]. A short alarum within.

2. Lord. Go tell the Count Rossillion and my brother,
    We have caught the woodcock, and will keep him
       muffled
    Till we do hear from them.

2. Soldier.   Captain, I will.

2. Lord. 'A will betray us all unto ourselves;
    Inform on that.

2. Soldier.   So I will, sir.   90

2. Lord. Till then I'll keep him dark and safely locked.

                          Exeunt.

70 *discover* reveal   78 *hoodwinked* blindfolded   79 *Haply* perhaps
83 *faithfully* in good faith   85 *space* time   87 *woodcock* (proverbially
foolish bird)

Enter Bertram and the Maid called Diana.

Bertram. They told me that your name was Fontybell.
Diana. No, my good lord, Diana.
Bertram.   Titled goddess,
   And worth it, with addition! But, fair soul,
   In your fine frame hath love no quality?
5   If the quick fire of youth light not your mind,
   You are no maiden, but a monument.
   When you are dead you should be such a one
   As you are now, for you are cold and stern;
   And now you should be as your mother was
10   When your sweet self was got.
Diana. She then was honest.
Bertram.   So should you be.
Diana.   No.
   My mother did but duty — such, my lord,
   As you owe to your wife.
Bertram.   No more o' that;
   I prithee do not strive against my vows.
15   I was compelled to her, but I love thee
   By love's own sweet constraint, and will forever
   Do thee all rights of service.
Diana.   Ay, so you serve us
   Till we serve you; but when you have our roses,
   You barely leave our thorns to prick ourselves,
   And mock us with our bareness.
20 *Bertram.*   How have I sworn!
Diana. 'Tis not the many oaths that makes the truth,
   But the plain single vow that is vowed true.

IV, ii, 3 *worth ... addition* deserving of that title, and more   5 *quick*
vital   10 *got* begotten   11 *honest* chaste   14 *vows* i.e. those sworn
against Helena

What is not holy, that we swear not by,
But take the High'st to witness; then pray you tell me,
If I should swear by Jove's great attributes   25
I loved you dearly, would you believe my oaths
When I did love you ill? This has no holding,
To swear by Him whom I protest to love,
That I will work against Him. Therefore your oaths
Are words, and poor conditions but unsealed —   30
At least in my opinion.
Bertram.   Change it, change it;
 Be not so holy-cruel; love is holy,
 And my integrity ne'er knew the crafts
 That you do charge men with. Stand no more off,
 But give thyself unto my sick desires,   35
 Who then recovers. Say thou art mine, and ever
 My love, as it begins, shall so persever.
Diana. I see that men may rope's in such a snare
 That we'll forsake ourselves. Give me that ring.
Bertram. I'll lend it thee, my dear, but have no power   40
 To give it from me.
Diana.   Will you not, my lord?
Bertram. It is an honor 'longing to our house,
 Bequeathèd down from many ancestors,
 Which were the greatest obloquy i' th' world
 In me to lose.
Diana.   Mine honor's such a ring;   45
 My chastity's the jewel of our house,
 Bequeathèd down from many ancestors,
 Which were the greatest obloquy i' th' world
 In me to lose. Thus your own proper wisdom

27 *ill* poorly, or not at all   *holding* consistency   28 *protest* promise
30 *poor ... unsealed* unworthy provisos without binding force (?)
42 *'longing* belonging   45 *honor* chastity   49 *proper* own

50   Brings in the champion Honor on my part
     Against your vain assault.
Bertram.   Here, take my ring!
     My house, mine honor, yea, my life be thine,
     And I'll be bid by thee.
Diana. When midnight comes, knock at my chamber
         window;
55   I'll order take my mother shall not hear.
     Now will I charge you in the band of truth,
     When you have conquered my yet maiden bed,
     Remain there but an hour, nor speak to me;
     My reasons are most strong, and you shall know them
60   When back again this ring shall be delivered.
     And on your finger in the night I'll put
     Another ring, that what in time proceeds
     May token to the future our past deeds.
     Adieu till then; then, fail not; you have won
65   A wife of me, though there my hope be done.
Bertram. A heaven on earth I have won by wooing thee.
                                        [Exit.]

Diana. For which live long to thank both heaven and me!
     You may so in the end.
     My mother told me just how he would woo,
70   As if she sat in 's heart. She says all men
     Have the like oaths. He had sworn to marry me
     When his wife 's dead; therefore I'll lie with him
     When I am buried. Since Frenchmen are so braid,
     Marry that will, I live and die a maid.
75   Only, in this disguise I think 't no sin
     To cozen him that would unjustly win.   *Exit.*

53 *bid* commanded   56 *band* bond   65 *done* lost   73 *braid* deceitful
74 *that* who   76 *cozen* cheat

*Enter the two French Captains and some two or three
Soldiers.*

2. *Lord.* You have not given him his mother's letter?

1. *Lord.* I have delivered it an hour since. There is something in't that stings his nature, for on the reading it he
changed almost into another man.

2. *Lord.* He has much worthy blame laid upon him for 5
shaking off so good a wife and so sweet a lady.

1. *Lord.* Especially he hath incurred the everlasting displeasure of the king, who had even tuned his bounty to
sing happiness to him. I will tell you a thing, but you
shall let it dwell darkly with you.   10

2. *Lord.* When you have spoken it, 'tis dead, and I am the
grave of it.

1. *Lord.* He hath perverted a young gentlewoman here in
Florence, of a most chaste renown, and this night he
fleshes his will in the spoil of her honor. He hath given 15
her his monumental ring, and thinks himself made in
the unchaste composition.

2. *Lord.* Now God delay our rebellion! As we are ourselves,
what things are we!

1. *Lord.* Merely our own traitors. And as in the common 20
course of all treasons, we still see them reveal themselves
till they attain to their abhorred ends, so he that in this
action contrives against his own nobility, in his proper
stream o'erflows himself.

IV, iii, 5 *worthy* deserved   15 *fleshes his will* gratifies his lust   *spoil*
ruin   *honor* chastity   16 *monumental* serving as a token of identity
made i.e. a made man   17 *unchaste composition* dishonorable bargain
18 *delay* mitigate   *rebellion* outbreaks of lust   *ourselves* unaided by
heaven   20 *Merely* entirely   21 *still* always   *reveal themselves* i.e.
for what they are   22 *abhorred ends* abhorrent objectives   23 *contrives*
plots   23–24 *in . . . himself* undoes himself with his own gifts

25 *2. Lord.* Is it not meant damnable in us to be trumpeters of
our unlawful intents? We shall not then have his company to-night?

1. Lord. Not till after midnight, for he is dieted to his hour.

2. Lord. That approaches apace. I would gladly have him
30 see his company anatomized, that he might take a measure of his own judgments, wherein so curiously he had
set this counterfeit.

1. Lord. We will not meddle with him till he come, for his
presence must be the whip of the other.

35 *2. Lord.* In the meantime, what hear you of these wars?

1. Lord. I hear there is an overture of peace.

2. Lord. Nay, I assure you, a peace concluded.

1. Lord. What will Count Rossillion do then? Will he
travel higher, or return again into France?

40 *2. Lord.* I perceive by this demand you are not altogether
of his council.

1. Lord. Let it be forbid, sir! So should I be a great deal of
his act.

2. Lord. Sir, his wife some two months since fled from his
45 house. Her pretense is a pilgrimage to Saint Jaques le
Grand; which holy undertaking with most austere sanc-
timony she accomplished; and there residing, the tender-
ness of her nature became as a prey to her grief; in fine,
made a groan of her last breath, and now she sings in
50 heaven.

1. Lord. How is this justified?

25 *meant damnable* a sign of damnation   28 *dieted* restricted   30 *company*
companion, i.e. Parolles   *anatomized* laid bare, exposed   30-31 *take . . .
judgments* appreciate his own misjudgment   31-32 *so . . . counterfeit* so
elaborately he had set this false jewel   33 *him* Parolles   *he* Bertram
his Bertram's   34 *the other* Parolles   39 *higher* farther   41 *of his council*
in his confidence   42-43 *of his act* responsible for his actions   45 *pretense*
intent   48 *in fine* at last   51 *justified* verified

2. Lord. The stronger part of it by her own letters, which makes her story true, even to the point of her death. Her death itself, which could not be her office to say is come, was faithfully confirmed by the rector of the place.   55

1. Lord. Hath the count all this intelligence?

2. Lord. Ay, and the particular confirmations, point from point, to the full arming of the verity.

1. Lord. I am heartily sorry that he'll be glad of this.

2. Lord. How mightily sometimes we make us comforts of   60 our losses!

1. Lord. And how mightily some other times we drown our gain in tears! The great dignity that his valor hath here acquired for him shall at home be encountered with a shame as ample.   65

2. Lord. The web of our life is of a mingled yarn, good and ill together; our virtues would be proud if our faults whipped them not, and our crimes would despair if they were not cherished by our virtues.

Enter a Messenger.

How now? Where's your master?   70

Messenger. He met the duke in the street, sir, of whom he hath taken a solemn leave; his lordship will next morning for France. The duke hath offered him letters of commendations to the king.   *[Exit.]*

2. Lord. They shall be no more than needful there, if they   75 were more than they can commend.

Enter [Bertram] Count Rossillion.

52 *stronger* larger 54 *which . . . come* which she could not herself report 58 *arming* corroboration 63 *gain* profits 75 *no . . . needful* i.e. of the utmost necessity 75–76 *if . . . commend* even if they outdid all possible commendation

1. Lord. They cannot be too sweet for the king's tartness. Here's his lordship now. How now, my lord, is't not after midnight?

80 *Bertram.* I have to-night dispatched sixteen businesses, a month's length apiece. By an abstract of success: I have congied with the duke, done my adieu with his nearest, buried a wife, mourned for her, writ to my lady mother I am returning, entertained my convoy, and between

85 these main parcels of dispatch effected many nicer needs. The last was the greatest, but that I have not ended yet.

2. Lord. If the business be of any difficulty, and this morning your departure hence, it requires haste of your lordship.

90 *Bertram.* I mean the business is not ended, as fearing to hear of it hereafter. But shall we have this dialogue between the Fool and the Soldier? Come, bring forth this counterfeit module has deceived me like a double-meaning prophesier.

95 *2. Lord.* Bring him forth. *[Exeunt Soldiers.]* Has sat i' th' stocks all night, poor gallant knave.

Bertram. No matter, his heels have deserved it, in usurping his spurs so long. How does he carry himself?

2. Lord. I have told your lordship already: the stocks carry

100 him. But to answer you as you would be understood, he weeps like a wench that had shed her milk; he hath confessed himself to Morgan, whom he supposes to be a friar, from the time of his remembrance to this very

81 *By ... success* to enumerate my successes 82 *congied with* taken leave of 84 *entertained my convoy* arranged my transportation 85 *parcels of dispatch* items of business *nicer* more delicate 86 *The last* i.e. the assignation with Diana 90–91 *as ... hear* since I fear I may hear 93 *module* mere image 93–94 *double-meaning* equivocating 96 *gallant* overdressed 101 *shed* spilled 103 *time ... remembrance* as far back as he can remember

instant disaster of his setting i' th' stocks. And what think
you he hath confessed?   105

Bertram. Nothing of me, has 'a?

2. Lord. His confession is taken, and it shall be read to his
face. If your lordship be in't, as I believe you are, you
must have the patience to hear it.

*Enter Parolles [guarded,] with [First Soldier as] his Inter-
preter.*

Bertram. A plague upon him! muffled! He can say nothing 110
of me.

1. Lord. Hush, hush! Hoodman comes! Portotartarossa.

Interpreter. He calls for the tortures; what will you say
without 'em?

Parolles. I will confess what I know without constraint. If 115
ye pinch me like a pasty, I can say no more.

Interpreter. Bosko chimurcho.

1. Lord. Boblibindo chicurmurco.

Interpreter. You are a merciful general. Our general bids
you answer to what I shall ask you out of a note.   120

Parolles. And truly, as I hope to live.

Interpreter. [reads] 'First demand of him how many horse
the duke is strong.' What say you to that?

Parolles. Five or six thousand, but very weak and unservice-
able. The troops are all scattered, and the commanders 125
very poor rogues, upon my reputation and credit, and
as I hope to live.

Interpreter. Shall I set down your answer so?

Parolles. Do. I'll take the sacrament on't, how and which
way you will.   130

Bertram. All's one to him. What a past-saving slave is this!

104 *instant* present 110 *muffled* blindfolded 116 *pasty* meat-pie 120 *note*
memorandum 131 *past-saving* damned

1. Lord. Y'are deceived, my lord. This is Monsieur Parolles, the gallant militarist – that was his own phrase – that had the whole theoric of war in the knot of his scarf, and the
135 practice in the chape of his dagger.

2. Lord. I will never trust a man again for keeping his sword clean, nor believe he can have everything in him by wearing his apparel neatly.

Interpreter. Well, that's set down.

140 *Parolles.* 'Five or six thousand horse,' I said – I will say true – 'or thereabouts' set down, for I'll speak truth.

1. Lord. He's very near the truth in this.

Bertram. But I con him no thanks for't, in the nature he delivers it.

145 *Parolles.* 'Poor rogues,' I pray you say.

Interpreter. Well, that's set down.

Parolles. I humbly thank you, sir; a truth's a truth – the rogues are marvellous poor.

Interpreter. [reads] 'Demand of him of what strength they
150 are afoot.' What say you to that?

Parolles. By my troth, sir, if I were to live this present hour, I will tell true. Let me see: Spurio, a hundred and fifty; Sebastian, so many; Corambus, so many; Jaques, so many; Guiltian, Cosmo, Lodowick, and Gratii, two
155 hundred fifty each; mine own company, Chitopher, Vaumond, Bentii, two hundred fifty each; so that the muster file, rotten and sound, upon my life amounts not to fifteen thousand poll, half of the which dare not shake the snow from off their cassocks, lest they shake them-
160 selves to pieces.

---

134 *theoric* theory 135 *chape* tip of the scabbard 138 *neatly* elegantly
143 *con* offer *in the nature* considering the manner 148 *marvellous* re-
markably 151 *live* i.e. live and die (?) 157 *file* roll 158 *poll* heads
159 *cassocks* cloaks

Bertram. What shall be done to him?

1. Lord. Nothing, but let him have thanks. Demand of him my condition, and what credit I have with the duke.

Interpreter. Well, that's set down. *[Reads]* 'You shall demand of him whether one Captain Dumain be i' th' 165 camp, a Frenchman; what his reputation is with the duke; what his valor, honesty, and expertness in wars; or whether he thinks it were not possible, with well-weighing sums of gold, to corrupt him to a revolt.' What say you to this? What do you know of it? 170

Parolles. I beseech you let me answer to the particular of the inter'gatories. Demand them singly.

Interpreter. Do you know this Captain Dumain?

Parolles. I know him. 'A was a botcher's prentice in Paris, from whence he was whipped for getting the shrieve's 175 fool with child—a dumb innocent, that could not say him nay. *[First Lord makes as if to strike him.]*

Bertram. Nay, by your leave, hold your hands, though I know his brains are forfeit to the next tile that falls.

Interpreter. Well, is this captain in the Duke of Florence's 180 camp?

Parolles. Upon my knowledge he is, and lousy.

1. Lord. Nay, look not so upon me; we shall hear of your lordship anon.

Interpreter. What is his reputation with the duke? 185

Parolles. The duke knows him for no other but a poor officer of mine, and writ to me this other day to turn him out o' th' band. I think I have his letter in my pocket.

Interpreter. Marry, we'll search.

168–69 *well-weighing* (1) heavy (2) apt to influence   172 *inter'gatories* questions   174 *botcher* cobbler, tailor   175–76 *shrieve's fool* feeble-minded person in the custody of the sheriff   176 *innocent* mental defective   179 *his . . . falls* he's in danger of death at any moment

190 *Parolles.* In good sadness, I do not know; either it is there, or it is upon a file with the duke's other letters in my tent.

Interpreter. Here 'tis; here's a paper; shall I read it to you?

Parolles. I do not know if it be it or no.

195 *Bertram.* Our interpreter does it well.

1. Lord. Excellently.

Interpreter. [*reads*] 'Dian, the count 's a fool, and full of gold.'

Parolles. That is not the duke's letter, sir; that is an adver- tisement to a proper maid in Florence, one Diana, to

200 take heed of the allurement of one Count Rossillion, a foolish idle boy, but for all that very ruttish. I pray you, sir, put it up again.

Interpreter. Nay, I'll read it first, by your favor.

Parolles. My meaning in't, I protest, was very honest in the

205 behalf of the maid; for I knew the young count to be a dangerous and lascivious boy, who is a whale to virginity, and devours up all the fry it finds.

Bertram. Damnable both-sides rogue!

Interpreter. [*reads*]

'When he swears oaths, bid him drop gold, and take it;

210 After he scores, he never pays the score.

Half-won is match well made; match, and well make it;

He ne'er pays after-debts, take it before.

And say a soldier, Dian, told thee this:

Men are to mell with, boys are not to kiss.

215 For count of this, the count 's a fool, I know it,

190 *sadness* earnest 191 *upon* in 198–99 *advertisement* warning 199 *proper* respectable 201 *ruttish* lecherous 207 *fry* i.e. unsuspecting victims 210 *scores* buys on credit *score* reckoning 211 *match well made* bargain well concluded 212 *after-debts* debts payable after the transaction is completed *it* Bertram's gold 214 *mell* have sexual intercourse 215 *count of* attend to

Who pays before, but not when he does owe it.
  Thine, as he vowed to thee in thine ear,
                                      PAROLLES.'

Bertram. He shall be whipped through the army with this
  rhyme in 's forehead.   220

2. Lord. This is your devoted friend, sir, the manifold
  linguist and the armipotent soldier.

Bertram. I could endure anything before but a cat, and now
  he's a cat to me.

Interpreter. I perceive, sir, by our general's looks, we shall 225
  be fain to hang you.

Parolles. My life, sir, in any case! Not that I am afraid to
  die, but that my offenses being many, I would repent
  out the remainder of nature. Let me live, sir, in a dun-
  geon, i' th' stocks, or anywhere, so I may live.   230

Interpreter. We'll see what may be done, so you confess
  freely. Therefore, once more to this Captain Dumain:
  you have answered to his reputation with the duke and
  to his valor. What is his honesty?

Parolles. He will steal, sir, an egg out of a cloister. For rapes 235
  and ravishments he parallels Nessus. He professes not
  keeping of oaths; in breaking 'em he is stronger than
  Hercules. He will lie, sir, with such volubility that you
  would think truth were a fool; drunkenness is his best
  virtue, for he will be swine-drunk, and in his sleep he   240
  does little harm, save to his bedclothes about him; but
  they know his conditions and lay him in straw. I have
  but little more to say, sir, of his honesty: he has everything that an honest man should not have; what an

221 *manifold* multiple   222 *armipotent* mighty in arms   226 *fain* obliged
229 *remainder of nature* rest of my natural life   236 *Nessus* centaur who tried
to rape Hercules' wife   *professes not* does not make a practice of   242
they i.e. other people   *conditions* disposition

245   honest man should have, he has nothing.

1. Lord. I begin to love him for this.

Bertram. For this description of thine honesty? A pox upon
    him! For me, he's more and more a cat.

Interpreter. What say you to his expertness in war?

250 *Parolles.* Faith, sir, has led the drum before the English
    tragedians — to belie him I will not — and more of his
    soldiership I know not, except in that country he had the
    honor to be the officer at a place there called Mile-end,
    to instruct for the doubling of files. I would do the man
255   what honor I can, but of this I am not certain.

1. Lord. He hath out-villained villainy so far that the rarity
    redeems him.

Bertram. A pox on him! He's a cat still.

Interpreter. His qualities being at this poor price, I need not
260   to ask you if gold will corrupt him to revolt.

Parolles. Sir, for a cardecue he will sell the fee simple of his
    salvation, the inheritance of it, and cut th' entail from all
    remainders, and a perpetual succession for it perpetually.

Interpreter. What's his brother, the other Captain Dumain?

265 *2. Lord.* Why does he ask him of me?

Interpreter. What's he?

Parolles. E'en a crow o' th' same nest; not altogether so
    great as the first in goodness, but greater a great deal in
    evil. He excels his brother for a coward, yet his brother
270   is reputed one of the best that is. In a retreat he outruns
    any lackey; marry, in coming on he has the cramp.

250–51 *led . . . tragedians* banged the drum to help advertise plays
253 *Mile-end* field in London where citizen recruits were drilled
254 *doubling of files* simple drill maneuvers 259 *qualities* virtues, abil-
ities 261 *cardecue* quart d'ecu, a small French coin *fee simple* absolute
and perpetual ownership 262 *entail* succession 263 *remainders* possible future heirs 271 *lackey* running footman *marry* indeed *coming
on* advancing, attacking

Interpreter. If your life be saved, will you undertake to
betray the Florentine?

Parolles. Ay, and the captain of his horse, Count Rossillion.

Interpreter. I'll whisper with the general, and know his 275
pleasure.

Parolles. [aside] I'll no more drumming; a plague of all
drums! Only to seem to deserve well, and to beguile the
supposition of that lascivious young boy, the count, have
I run into this danger; yet who would have suspected an 280
ambush where I was taken?

Interpreter. There is no remedy, sir, but you must die. The
general says, you that have so traitorously discovered the
secrets of your army, and made such pestiferous reports
of men very nobly held, can serve the world for no 285
honest use; therefore you must die. Come, headsman,
off with his head!

Parolles. O Lord, sir, let me live, or let me see my death!

Interpreter. That shall you, and take your leave of all your
friends.   *[Unmuffles him.]*

So, look about you. Know you any here?   290

Bertram. Good morrow, noble captain.

2. Lord. God bless you, Captain Parolles.

1. Lord. God save you, noble captain.

2. Lord. Captain, what greeting will you to my Lord
Lafew? I am for France.   295

1. Lord. Good captain, will you give me a copy of the
sonnet you writ to Diana in behalf of the Count Rossillion? An I were not a very coward, I'd compel it of you;
but fare you well.

Exeunt [Bertram and Lords].

278–79 *beguile the supposition* deceive the imaginings 283 *discovered*
disclosed 284 *pestiferous* mischievous 285 *held* esteemed 298 *An* if
very perfect

300 *Interpreter.* You are undone, captain — all but your scarf;
that has a knot on't yet.

Parolles. Who cannot be crushed with a plot?

Interpreter. If you could find out a country where but
women were that had received so much shame, you
305 might begin an impudent nation. Fare ye well, sir; I am
for France too; we shall speak of you there.

Exit [with Soldiers].

Parolles. Yet am I thankful. If my heart were great,
'Twould burst at this. Captain I'll be no more,
But I will eat and drink and sleep as soft
310 As captain shall. Simply the thing I am
Shall make me live. Who knows himself a braggart,
Let him fear this; for it will come to pass
That every braggart shall be found an ass.
Rust, sword! cool, blushes! and, Parolles, live
315 Safest in shame; being fooled, by foolery thrive.
There's place and means for every man alive.
I'll after them. *Exit.*

IV, iv   *Enter Helena, Widow, and Diana.*

Helena. That you may well perceive I have not wronged
you,
One of the greatest in the Christian world
Shall be my surety; 'fore whose throne 'tis needful,
Ere I can perfect mine intents, to kneel.
5 Time was I did him a desirèd office,
Dear almost as his life; which gratitude

315 *fooled* proved a fool   *foolery* folly   IV, iv, 3 *surety* guarantee
6 *which gratitude* gratitude for which

Through flinty Tartar's bosom would peep forth
And answer thanks. I duly am informed
His grace is at Marseilles, to which place
We have convenient convoy. You must know   10
I am supposèd dead; the army breaking,
My husband hies him home, where, heaven aiding,
And by the leave of my good lord the king,
We'll be before our welcome.

Widow.   Gentle madam,
You never had a servant to whose trust   15
Your business was more welcome.

Helena.   Nor you, mistress,
Ever a friend whose thoughts more truly labor
To recompense your love. Doubt not but heaven
Hath brought me up to be your daughter's dower,
As it hath fated her to be my motive   20
And helper to a husband. But, O strange men!
That can such sweet use make of what they hate,
When saucy trusting of the cozened thoughts
Defiles the pitchy night; so lust doth play
With what it loathes, for that which is away.   25
But more of this hereafter. You, Diana,
Under my poor instructions yet must suffer
Something in my behalf.

Diana.   Let death and honesty
Go with your impositions, I am yours
Upon your will to suffer.

Helena.   Yet, I pray you.   30

9 *Marseilles* (a trisyllable, spelled *Marcellus* in the folio)   11 *breaking*
disbanding   14 *be before* arrive ahead of   20 *motive* means, agent (?)
23–24 *When ... night* when wanton yielding to the deceptions of lust
makes black night even blacker   25 *for* in place of   28–30 *Let ... suffer*
so long as your instructions allow me to preserve my honor, I am ready to
die at your command   30 *Yet* a while longer

But with the word the time will bring on summer,
When briars shall have leaves as well as thorns,
And be as sweet as sharp. We must away;
Our wagon is prepared, and time revives us.
35   All's well that ends well; still the fine 's the crown.
Whate'er the course, the end is the renown.   *Exeunt.*

IV, v   *Enter [Lavatch, the] Clown, Old Lady [Countess], and*
        Lafew.

Lafew. No, no, no, your son was misled with a snipped-
taffeta fellow there, whose villainous saffron would have
made all the unbaked and doughy youth of a nation in
his color. Your daughter-in-law had been alive at this
5   hour, and your son here at home, more advanced by the
king than by that red-tailed humblebee I speak of.
Countess. I would I had not known him; it was the death
of the most virtuous gentlewoman that ever nature had
praise for creating. If she had partaken of my flesh and
10   cost me the dearest groans of a mother, I could not have
owed her a more rooted love.
Lafew. 'Twas a good lady, 'twas a good lady. We may
pick a thousand sallets ere we light on such another herb.
Lavatch. Indeed, sir, she was the sweet marjoram of the
15   sallet, or rather, the herb of grace.
Lafew. They are not herbs, you knave; they are nose herbs.

---

31 *with the word* upon the delivery of my letter (?)   34 *wagon* carriage
35 *fine* end IV, v, 1–2 *snipped-taffeta* slashed silk, both gaudy and flimsy
2 *saffron* yellow dye 3 *unbaked* i.e. half-baked *doughy* raw 6 *red-
tailed humblebee* brightly colored bumblebee 10 *dearest* direst 13 *sallets*
salads 15 *herb of grace* rue 16 *not herbs* not edible plants *nose herbs*
aromatic plants

Lavatch. I am no great Nebuchadnezzar, sir; I have not much skill in grass.

Lafew. Whether dost thou profess thyself, a knave or a fool?   20

Lavatch. A fool, sir, at a woman's service, and a knave at a man's.

Lafew. Your distinction?

Lavatch. I would cozen the man of his wife, and do his service.   25

Lafew. So you were a knave at his service indeed.

Lavatch. And I would give his wife my bauble, sir, to do her service.

Lafew. I will subscribe for thee, thou art both knave and fool.   30

Lavatch. At your service.

Lafew. No, no, no!

Lavatch. Why, sir, if I cannot serve you, I can serve as great a prince as you are.

Lafew. Who's that? a Frenchman?   35

Lavatch. Faith, sir, 'a has an English name, but his fisnomy is more hotter in France than there.

Lafew. What prince is that?

Lavatch. The Black Prince, sir, alias the prince of darkness, alias the devil.   40

Lafew. Hold thee, there's my purse. I give thee not this to suggest thee from thy master thou talk'st of; serve him still.

Lavatch. I am a woodland fellow, sir, that always loved a

---

17 *I ... Nebuchadnezzar* I do not have a nose like an emperor's   18 *grass* (with pun on 'grace')   19 *Whether* which   24–25 *do his service* take his place sexually   27 *bauble* coxcomb (with sexual double-entendre)   29 *subscribe* vouch   36 *fisnomy* physiognomy   39 *Black Prince* nickname of the eldest son of Edward III, hence the 'English name' of l. 36   42 *suggest* lure   43 *still* ever

45   great fire, and the master I speak of ever keeps a good
fire. But sure he is the prince of the world; let his nobility
remain in 's court; I am for the house with the narrow
gate, which I take to be too little for pomp to enter.
Some that humble themselves may, but the many will be
50   too chill and tender, and they'll be for the flowery way
that leads to the broad gate and the great fire.

Lafew. Go thy ways; I begin to be aweary of thee; and I
tell thee so before, because I would not fall out with thee.
Go thy ways; let my horses be well looked to, without
55   any tricks.

Lavatch. If I put any tricks upon 'em, sir, they shall be
jades' tricks, which are their own right by the law of
nature.   *Exit.*

Lafew. A shrewd knave and an unhappy.

60 *Countess.* So 'a is. My lord that's gone made himself much
sport out of him. By his authority he remains here,
which he thinks is a patent for his sauciness; and indeed
he has no pace, but runs where he will.

Lafew. I like him well; 'tis not amiss. And I was about to
65   tell you, since I heard of the good lady's death, and that
my lord your son was upon his return home, I moved
the king my master to speak in the behalf of my daughter;
which, in the minority of them both, his majesty out of
a self-gracious remembrance did first propose. His high-
70   ness hath promised me to do it; and to stop up the
displeasure he hath conceived against your son there is
no fitter matter. How does your ladyship like it?

---

49 *many* multitude   50 *chill and tender* susceptible to cold   53 *before*
beforehand   57 *jades' tricks* mischievous tricks   59 *shrewd* sharp-tongued
63 *has no pace* is unrestrained   69 *self-gracious remembrance* unprompted
generosity   70 *stop up* put a stop to

Countess. With very much content, my lord, and I wish
it happily effected.

Lafew. His highness comes post from Marseilles, of as able 75
body as when he numbered thirty; 'a will be here to-
morrow, or I am deceived by him that in such intelligence hath seldom failed.

Countess. It rejoices me that I hope I shall see him ere I die.
I have letters that my son will be here to-night. I shall 80
beseech your lordship to remain with me till they meet
together.

Lafew. Madam, I was thinking with what manners I might
safely be admitted.

Countess. You need but plead your honorable privilege. 85

Lafew. Lady, of that I have made a bold charter, but I
thank my God it holds yet.

Enter [Lavatch, the] Clown.

Lavatch. O madam, yonder's my lord your son with a
patch of velvet on 's face. Whether there be a scar under 't
or no, the velvet knows, but 'tis a goodly patch of velvet; 90
his left cheek is a cheek of two pile and a half, but his
right cheek is worn bare.

Lafew. A scar nobly got, or a noble scar, is a good livery
of honor; so belike is that.

Lavatch. But it is your carbonadoed face. 95

Lafew. Let us go see your son, I pray you. I long to talk
with the young noble soldier.

Lavatch. Faith, there's a dozen of 'em, with delicate fine

76 *numbered thirty* was thirty years old   85 *honorable privilege* privilege
due your honor   86 *charter* license   91 *two ... half* especially thick
velvet   92 *worn bare* unpatched   95 *carbonadoed* slashed (to drain vene-
real ulcers)

hats, and most courteous feathers which bow the head
100   and nod at every man.   *Exeunt.*

V, i   *Enter Helena, Widow, and Diana, with two Attendants.*

   Helena. But this exceeding posting day and night
     Must wear your spirits low. We cannot help it;
     But since you have made the days and nights as one,
     To wear your gentle limbs in my affairs,
5   Be bold you do so grow in my requital
     As nothing can unroot you.

              Enter a Gentleman.

                    In happy time –
     This man may help me to his majesty's ear,
     If he would spend his power. God save you, sir!
   Gentleman. And you.
10 *Helena.* Sir, I have seen you in the court of France.
   Gentleman. I have been sometimes there.
   Helena. I do presume, sir, that you are not fall'n
     From the report that goes upon your goodness;
     And therefore, goaded with most sharp occasions,
15   Which lay nice manners by, I put you to
     The use of your own virtues, for the which
     I shall continue thankful.
   Gentleman.   What's your will?
   Helena. That it will please you
     To give this poor petition to the king,
20   And aid me with that store of power you have
     To come into his presence.

V, i, 1 *posting* riding   5 *bold* assured   *requital* thankfulness   15 *nice*
scrupulous   15–16 *I . . . virtues* I help you put your goodness into action

Gentleman. The king 's not here.

Helena.   Not here, sir?

Gentleman.   Not indeed;
 He hence removed last night, and with more haste
 Than is his use.

Widow.   Lord, how we lose our pains!

Helena. All's well that ends well yet,   25
 Though time seem so adverse and means unfit.
 I do beseech you, whither is he gone?

Gentleman. Marry, as I take it, to Rossillion,
 Whither I am going.

Helena.   I do beseech you, sir,
 Since you are like to see the king before me, 30
 Commend the paper to his gracious hand,
 Which I presume shall render you no blame,
 But rather make you thank your pains for it.
 I will come after you with what good speed
 Our means will make us means.

Gentleman.   This I'll do for you. 35

Helena. And you shall find yourself to be well thanked,
 Whate'er falls more. — We must to horse again.
 Go, go, provide.   *[Exeunt.]*

Enter [Lavatch, the] Clown, and Parolles. V, ii

Parolles. Good Master Lavatch, give my Lord Lafew this
 letter. I have ere now, sir, been better known to you,
 when I have held familiarity with fresher clothes; but I
 am now, sir, muddied in Fortune's mood, and smell
 somewhat strong of her strong displeasure.   5

Lavatch. Truly, Fortune's displeasure is but sluttish if it

35 *Our means ... means* our resources will permit V, ii, 4 *mood* anger

smell so strongly as thou speak'st of; I will henceforth
eat no fish of Fortune's buttering. Prithee, allow the
wind!

10 *Parolles.* Nay, you need not to stop your nose, sir; I spake
but by a metaphor.

Lavatch. Indeed, sir, if your metaphor stink, I will stop my
nose, or against any man's metaphor. Prithee, get thee
further.

15 *Parolles.* Pray you, sir, deliver me this paper.

Lavatch. Foh! prithee, stand away! A paper from Fortune's
close-stool, to give to a nobleman! Look, here he comes
himself.

Enter Lafew.

Here is a pur of Fortune's, sir, or of Fortune's cat — but
20 not a musk-cat — that has fallen into the unclean fishpond
of her displeasure, and, as he says, is muddied withal.
Pray you, sir, use the carp as you may, for he looks like
a poor decayed, ingenious, foolish, rascally knave. I do
pity his distress in my similes of comfort, and leave him
25 to your lordship. *[Exit.]*

Parolles. My lord, I am a man whom Fortune hath cruelly
scratched.

Lafew. And what would you have me to do? 'Tis too late
to pare her nails now. Wherein have you played the
30 knave with Fortune that she should scratch you, who of
herself is a good lady, and would not have knaves thrive
long under her? There's a cardecue for you. Let the

8 *of Fortune's buttering* served up by Fortune   8–9 *allow the wind* stand
aside   17 *close-stool* privy   19 *pur* knave (in cards, with pun on 'purr')
20 *musk-cat* (prized for its scent)   22 *carp* inhabitant of 'unclean fish-
ponds,' and a proverbial chatterer   23 *ingenious* inept (?)

justices make you and Fortune friends; I am for other
business.

Parolles. I beseech your honor to hear me one single word. 35

Lafew. You beg a single penny more. Come, you shall ha't;
save your word.

Parolles. My name, my good lord, is Parolles.

Lafew. You beg more than word then. Cox my passion!
Give me your hand. How does your drum?   40

Parolles. O my good lord, you were the first that found me.

Lafew. Was I, in sooth? And I was the first that lost thee.

Parolles. It lies in you, my lord, to bring me in some
grace, for you did bring me out.

Lafew. Out upon thee, knave! Dost thou put upon me at 45
once both the office of God and the devil? One brings
thee in grace, and the other brings thee out. *[Trumpets
sound.]* The king's coming; I know by his trumpets.
Sirrah, inquire further after me; I had talk of you last
night; though you are a fool and a knave, you shall eat. 50
Go to; follow.

Parolles. I praise God for you.   *[Exeunt.]*

Flourish. Enter King, Old Lady [Countess], Lafew, the   V, iii
two French Lords, with Attendants.

King. We lost a jewel of her, and our esteem
Was made much poorer by it; but your son,
As mad in folly, lacked the sense to know
Her estimation home.

---

33 *justices* (under Elizabethan law, responsible for beggars) 39 *more
than word* i.e. many words, 'Parolles' *Cox* God's   V, iii, 1 *our esteem* our
own value   3–4 *know ... home* appreciate her worth to the full

Countess.   'Tis past, my liege,
5   And I beseech your majesty to make it
     Natural rebellion, done i' th' blade of youth,
     When oil and fire, too strong for reason's force,
     O'erbears it and burns on.

King.   My honored lady,
     I have forgiven and forgotten all,
10   Though my revenges were high bent upon him,
     And watched the time to shoot.

Lafew.   This I must say —
     But first I beg my pardon — the young lord
     Did to his majesty, his mother, and his lady,
     Offense of mighty note, but to himself
15   The greatest wrong of all. He lost a wife
     Whose beauty did astonish the survey
     Of richest eyes, whose words all ears took captive,
     Whose dear perfection hearts that scorned to serve
     Humbly called mistress.

King.   Praising what is lost
20   Makes the remembrance dear. Well, call him hither;
     We are reconciled, and the first view shall kill
     All repetition. Let him not ask our pardon;
     The nature of his great offense is dead,
     And deeper than oblivion we do bury
25   Th' incensing relics of it. Let him approach,
     A stranger, no offender; and inform him
     So 'tis our will he should.

Gentleman.   I shall, my liege.   *[Exit.]*

---

6 *blade* i.e. greenness, callowness   10 *high bent* grimly aimed   11 *watched the time* waited for the right moment   17 *richest* most experienced   22 *repetition* rehearsing of past grievances   23 *The . . . dead* the particular wrongs he committed are forgotten   25 *relics* reminders

King. What says he to your daughter? Have you spoke?
Lafew. All that he is hath reference to your highness.
King. Then shall we have a match. I have letters sent me   30
    That sets him high in fame.

Enter Count Bertram.

Lafew.   He looks well on't.
King. I am not a day of season,
    For thou mayst see a sunshine and a hail
    In me at once. But to the brightest beams
    Distracted clouds give way; so stand thou forth,   35
    The time is fair again.
Bertram.   My high-repented blames,
    Dear sovereign, pardon to me.
King.   All is whole;
    Not one word more of the consumèd time.
    Let's take the instant by the forward top;
    For we are old, and on our quick'st decrees   40
    Th' inaudible and noiseless foot of time
    Steals ere we can effect them. You remember
    The daughter of this lord?
Bertram. Admiringly, my liege. At first
    I stuck my choice upon her, ere my heart   45
    Durst make too bold a herald of my tongue;
    Where the impression of mine eye infixing,
    Contempt his scornful perspective did lend me,
    Which warped the line of every other favor,
    Scorned a fair color or expressed it stol'n,   50

29 *hath reference to* submits himself to   32 *of season* of any one season,
i.e. of steady weather   39 *forward top* forelock   47 *Where* i.e. upon
Lafew's daughter   48 *perspective* distorting optical glass   49 *warped
. . . favor* made the features of all other faces seem ugly   50 *color* com-
plexion   *expressed it stol'n* declared it artificial

Extended or contracted all proportions
To a most hideous object. Thence it came
That she whom all men praised, and whom myself,
Since I have lost, have loved, was in mine eye
The dust that did offend it.

55 *King.*   Well excused;
That thou didst love her strikes some scores away
From the great compt. But love that comes too late,
Like a remorseful pardon slowly carried,
To the great sender turns a sour offense,

60 Crying, 'That's good that's gone.' Our rash faults
Make trivial price of serious things we have,
Not knowing them until we know their grave.
Oft our displeasures, to ourselves unjust,
Destroy our friends, and after weep their dust;

65 Our own love, waking, cries to see what's done,
While shameful hate sleeps out the afternoon.
Be this sweet Helen's knell, and now forget her.
Send forth your amorous token for fair Maudlin.
The main consents are had, and here we'll stay

70 To see our widower's second marriage day.
Countess. Which better than the first, O dear heaven, bless,
Or, ere they meet, in me, O nature, cesse!
Lafew. Come on, my son, in whom my house's name
Must be digested, give a favor from you

75 To sparkle in the spirits of my daughter,

51–52 *Extended ... object* stretched out or cramped together all other forms till they appeared hideous 53 *she* Helena 57 *compt* account 59 *turns ... offense* goes sour on him 62 *Not ... grave* not appreciating them till we've lost them for good 63 *displeasures* offenses 64 *weep their dust* mourn over their ashes 65 *waking* belatedly coming to its senses 66 *hate sleeps* i.e. having sated itself by destroying the friend, while love slept 72 *they* the two marriages *meet* resemble each other *cesse* cease 74 *digested* assimilated *favor* love-token

That she may quickly come.   *[Bertram gives him a ring.]*
                     By my old beard
And every hair that's on't, Helen that's dead
Was a sweet creature; such a ring as this,
The last that e'er I took her leave at court,
I saw upon her finger.

Bertram.   Hers it was not.   80
King. Now pray you let me see it; for mine eye,
    While I was speaking, oft was fastened to't.
                         [Takes the ring.]
    This ring was mine, and when I gave it Helen
    I bade her, if her fortunes ever stood
    Necessitied to help, that by this token   85
    I would relieve her. Had you that craft to reave her
    Of what should stead her most?

Bertram.   My gracious sovereign,
    Howe'er it pleases you to take it so,
    The ring was never hers.

Countess.   Son, on my life,
    I have seen her wear it, and she reckoned it   90
    At her life's rate.

Lafew.   I am sure I saw her wear it.
Bertram. You are deceived, my lord; she never saw it.
    In Florence was it from a casement thrown me,
    Wrapped in a paper, which contained the name
    Of her that threw it. Noble she was, and thought   95
    I stood engaged; but when I had subscribed
    To mine own fortune, and informed her fully
    I could not answer in that course of honor
    As she had made the overture, she ceased

---

79 *last ... leave* last time I took leave of her 85 *Necessitied to* in need of 86 *reave* despoil 87 *stead* aid 96–97 *subscribed ... fortune* explained my situation 98 *answer ... honor* commit myself to the same degree

100   In heavy satisfaction, and would never
       Receive the ring again.

   King.   Plutus himself,
       That knows the tinct and multiplying med'cine,
       Hath not in nature's mystery more science
       Than I have in this ring. 'Twas mine, 'twas Helen's,
105   Whoever gave it you. Then if you know
       That you are well acquainted with yourself,
       Confess 'twas hers, and by what rough enforcement
       You got it from her. She called the saints to surety
       That she would never put it from her finger
110   Unless she gave it to yourself in bed —
       Where you have never come — or sent it us
       Upon her great disaster.

   Bertram.   She never saw it.

   King. Thou speak'st it falsely, as I love mine honor,
       And mak'st conjectural fears to come into me
115   Which I would fain shut out. If it should prove
       That thou art so inhuman — 'twill not prove so,
       And yet I know not — thou didst hate her deadly,
       And she is dead; which nothing but to close
       Her eyes myself could win me to believe,
120   More than to see this ring. Take him away.

                 [Attendants arrest Bertram.]
       My forepast proofs, howe'er the matter fall,
       Shall tax my fears of little vanity,
       Having vainly feared too little. Away with him;
       We'll sift this matter further.

---

100 *In heavy satisfaction* disappointed but convinced   101 *Plutus* god of riches   102 *tinct ... medicine* elixir for converting base metals to gold 103 *science* knowledge   105–6 *if ... yourself* if you know what's good for you (?)   112 *Upon ... disaster* in time of direst peril   121 *forepast proofs* ills already undergone   122 *tax ... vanity* suffice to establish the legitimacy of my fears   123 *vainly* foolishly

Bertram.   If you shall prove
   This ring was ever hers, you shall as easy   125
   Prove that I husbanded her bed in Florence,
   Where yet she never was.   *[Exit, guarded.]*
King. I am wrapped in dismal thinkings.

               Enter a Gentleman.

Gentleman.   Gracious sovereign,
   Whether I have been to blame or no, I know not:
   Here's a petition from a Florentine,   130
   Who hath for four or five removes come short
   To tender it herself. I undertook it,
   Vanquished thereto by the fair grace and speech
   Of the poor suppliant, who by this, I know,
   Is here attending. Her business looks in her   135
   With an importing visage, and she told me,
   In a sweet verbal brief, it did concern
   Your highness with herself.
[King reads] a letter. 'Upon his many protestations to marry
   me when his wife was dead, I blush to say it, he won me. 140
   Now is the Count Rossillion a widower, his vows are
   forfeited to me, and my honor's paid to him. He stole
   from Florence, taking no leave, and I follow him to his
   country for justice: grant it me, O king! In you it best
   lies; otherwise a seducer flourishes, and a poor maid is 145
   undone.
                         DIANA CAPILET.'
Lafew. I will buy me a son-in-law in a fair, and toll for
   this. I'll none of him.

131 *removes* changes of residence of the court   132 *tender* offer   135
looks manifests itself   136 *importing* urgent   137 *verbal brief* oral mes-
sage   148 *in a fair* (where cheap and stolen goods are sold)   *toll for*
get rid of

150 *King.* The heavens have thought well on thee, Lafew,
   To bring forth this discov'ry. Seek these suitors.
   Go speedily, and bring again the count.
                    [*Exeunt Gentleman and an Attendant.*]
   I am afeard the life of Helen, lady,
   Was foully snatched.
Countess.   Now justice on the doers!

                    Enter Bertram, [guarded].

155 *King.* I wonder, sir, sith wives are monsters to you,
   And that you fly them as you swear them lordship,
   Yet you desire to marry.

                    Enter Widow [and] Diana.

                         What woman's that?
Diana. I am, my lord, a wretched Florentine,
   Derivèd from the ancient Capilet.
160 My suit, as I do understand, you know,
   And therefore know how far I may be pitied.
Widow. I am her mother, sir, whose age and honor
   Both suffer under this complaint we bring,
   And both shall cease, without your remedy.
165 *King.* Come hither, count; do you know these women?
Bertram. My lord, I neither can nor will deny
   But that I know them. Do they charge me further?
Diana. Why do you look so strange upon your wife?
Bertram. She's none of mine, my lord.
Diana.   If you shall marry,
170 You give away this hand, and that is mine;
   You give away heaven's vows, and those are mine;
   You give away myself, which is known mine;

---

155 *sith* since   156 *swear them lordship* promise them marriage   159 *Derivèd*
descended   170 *this hand* Bertram's

For I by vow am so embodied yours
That she which marries you must marry me —
Either both or none.   175

Lafew. Your reputation comes too short for my daughter;
  you are no husband for her.

Bertram. My lord, this is a fond and desp'rate creature,
  Whom sometime I have laughed with; let your highness
  Lay a more noble thought upon mine honor   180
  Than for to think that I would sink it here.

King. Sir, for my thoughts, you have them ill to friend
  Till your deeds gain them. Fairer prove your honor
  Than in my thought it lies!

Diana.   Good my lord,
  Ask him upon his oath if he does think   185
  He had not my virginity.

King. What say'st thou to her?

Bertram.   She's impudent, my lord,
  And was a common gamester to the camp.

Diana. He does me wrong, my lord. If I were so,
  He might have bought me at a common price.   190
  Do not believe him. O, behold this ring,
  Whose high respect and rich validity
  Did lack a parallel; yet for all that
  He gave it to a commoner o' th' camp,
  If I be one.

Countess.   He blushes, and 'tis it.   195
  Of six preceding ancestors, that gem,
  Conferred by testament to th' sequent issue,
  Hath it been owed and worn. This is his wife;
  That ring's a thousand proofs.

---

173 *embodied yours* united to you 178 *fond* foolish 179 *sometime* formerly 188 *gamester* lewd person 192 *respect* worth *validity* value
197 *sequent issue* next generation 198 *owed* owned

King.   Methought you said
200   You saw one here in court could witness it.
Diana. I did, my lord, but loath am to produce
      So bad an instrument; his name 's Parolles.
Lafew. I saw the man to-day, if man he be.
King. Find him and bring him hither. *[Exit an Attendant.]*
Bertram.   What of him?
205   He's quoted for a most perfidious slave,
      With all the spots o' th' world taxed and deboshed,
      Whose nature sickens but to speak a truth.
      Am I or that or this for what he'll utter,
      That will speak anything?
King.   She hath that ring of yours.
210 *Bertram.* I think she has. Certain it is I liked her,
      And boarded her i' th' wanton way of youth.
      She knew her distance and did angle for me,
      Madding my eagerness with her restraint —
      As all impediments in fancy's course
215   Are motives of more fancy — and in fine
      Her infinite cunning with her modern grace
      Subdued me to her rate. She got the ring,
      And I had that which any inferior might
      At market price have bought.
Diana.   I must be patient.
220   You that have turned off a first so noble wife
      May justly diet me. I pray you yet —
      Since you lack virtue, I will lose a husband —
      Send for your ring, I will return it home,
      And give me mine again.

205 *quoted* noted 206 *taxed and deboshed* charged with debauchery
211 *boarded* accosted 213 *Madding* spurring 214 *in fancy's course* in
amorous pursuit 215 *fancy* erotic fantasies *in fine* at length 216 *modern*
commonplace 217 *Subdued . . . rate* made me accept her terms 221 *diet*
restrain

Bertram.   I have it not.

King. What ring was yours, I pray you?

Diana.   Sir, much like   225
   The same upon your finger.

King. Know you this ring? This ring was his of late.

Diana. And this was it I gave him, being abed.

King. The story then goes false, you threw it him
   Out of a casement?

Diana.   I have spoke the truth.   230

Enter Parolles.

Bertram. My lord, I do confess the ring was hers.

King. You boggle shrewdly; every feather starts you.
   Is this the man you speak of?

Diana.   Ay, my lord.

King. Tell me, sirrah — but tell me true, I charge you,
   Not fearing the displeasure of your master,   235
   Which, on your just proceeding, I'll keep off —
   By him and by this woman here what know you?

Parolles. So please your majesty, my master hath been an
   honorable gentleman. Tricks he hath had in him, which
   gentlemen have.   240

King. Come, come, to th' purpose. Did he love this
   woman?

Parolles. Faith, sir, he did love her; but how?

King. How, I pray you?

Parolles. He did love her, sir, as a gentleman loves a   245
   woman.

King. How is that?

Parolles. He loved her, sir, and loved her not.

232 *boggle shrewdly* shy nervously *starts* startles 236 *on ... proceeding*
if you tell the truth 237 *By* concerning

137

King. As thou art a knave, and no knave. What an equiv-
250   ocal companion is this!

Parolles. I am a poor man, and at your majesty's command.

Lafew. He's a good drum, my lord, but a naughty orator.

Diana. Do you know he promised me marriage?

Parolles. Faith, I know more than I'll speak.

255 *King.* But wilt thou not speak all thou know'st?

Parolles. Yes, so please your majesty. I did go between
   them as I said; but more than that, he loved her — for
   indeed he was mad for her, and talked of Satan and of
   Limbo and of Furies and I know not what. Yet I was
260   in that credit with them at that time that I knew of their
   going to bed, and of other motions, as promising her
   marriage, and things which would derive me ill will to
   speak of; therefore I will not speak what I know.

King. Thou hast spoken all already, unless thou canst say
265   they are married; but thou art too fine in thy evidence;
   therefore stand aside.

   This ring you say was yours?

Diana.   Ay, my good lord.

King. Where did you buy it? or who gave it you?

Diana. It was not given me, nor I did not buy it.

King. Who lent it you?

270 *Diana.*   It was not lent me neither.

King. Where did you find it then?

Diana.   I found it not.

King. If it were yours by none of all these ways,
   How could you give it him?

Diana.   I never gave it him.

Lafew. This woman's an easy glove, my lord; she goes
275   off and on at pleasure.

250 *companion* rascal   252 *drum* drummer   *naughty* wicked   261 *motions*
proposals   262 *derive* gain   265 *fine* subtle

King. This ring was mine; I gave it his first wife.
Diana. It might be yours or hers for aught I know.
King. Take her away, I do not like her now;
    To prison with her, and away with him.
    Unless thou tell'st me where thou hadst this ring,   280
    Thou diest within this hour.
Diana.   I'll never tell you.
King. Take her away.
Diana.   I'll put in bail, my liege.
King. I think thee now some common customer.
Diana. By Jove, if ever I knew man, 'twas you.
King. Wherefore hast thou accused him all this while?   285
Diana. Because he's guilty, and he is not guilty.
    He knows I am no maid, and he'll swear to't;
    I'll swear I am a maid and he knows not.
    Great king, I am no strumpet, by my life;
    I am either maid, or else this old man's wife.   290
                    [Points to Lafew.]
King. She does abuse our ears; to prison with her!
Diana. Good mother, fetch my bail. Stay, royal sir,
                    [Exit Widow.]

    The jeweller that owes the ring is sent for,
    And he shall surety me. But for this lord,
    Who hath abused me, as he knows himself,   295
    Though yet he never harmed me, here I quit him.
    He knows himself my bed he hath defiled,
    And at that time he got his wife with child.
    Dead though she be, she feels her young one kick.
    So there's my riddle: one that's dead is quick —   300
    And now behold the meaning.

---

283 *customer* prostitute 293 *owes* owns 294 *surety me* be my security
296 *quit* acquit, release 300 *quick* alive

Enter Helena and Widow.

King.   Is there no exorcist
   Beguiles the truer office of mine eyes?
   Is't real that I see?
Helena.   No, my good lord,
   'Tis but the shadow of a wife you see,
   The name and not the thing.
305 **Bertram.**   Both, both; O, pardon!
   Helena. O my good lord, when I was like this maid
   I found you wondrous kind. There is your ring,
   And look you, here's your letter. This it says:
   'When from my finger you can get this ring,
310   And are by me with child,' etc. This is done.
   Will you be mine, now you are doubly won?
Bertram. If she, my liege, can make me know this clearly,
   I'll love her dearly—ever, ever dearly.
Helena. If it appear not plain, and prove untrue,
315   Deadly divorce step between me and you.
   O my dear mother, do I see you living?
Lafew. Mine eyes smell onions; I shall weep anon.
   [*To Parolles*] Good Tom Drum, lend me a handkercher.
      So,
   I thank thee. Wait on me home; I'll make sport with thee.
320   Let thy curtsies alone; they are scurvy ones.
King. Let us from point to point this story know,
   To make the even truth in pleasure flow.
   [*To Diana*] If thou beest yet a fresh uncroppèd flower,
   Choose thou thy husband, and I'll pay thy dower;
325   For I can guess that by thy honest aid
   Thou kept'st a wife herself, thyself a maid.

301 *exorcist* magician   302 *Beguiles ... office* deceives the true vision
320 *curtsies* reverences   322 *even* exact

Of that and all the progress more and less
Resolvedly more leisure shall express.
All yet seems well, and if it end so meet,
The bitter past, more welcome is the sweet.   *Flourish.* 330

[EPILOGUE]

The king's a beggar, now the play is done.
All is well ended if this suit be won,
That you express content; which we will pay
With strife to please you, day exceeding day.
Ours be your patience then, and yours our parts;   335
Your gentle hands lend us, and take our hearts.

Exeunt omnes.

328 *Resolvedly* with full explanation 329 *meet* fittingly 333 *express content* i.e. by applause 334 *strife* effort 335 *Ours ... parts* we will become the audience (to your applause) while you become the actors (by applauding)

Appendix: List of Emendations

Apart from relineation, the following emendations constitute the only material departures from the folio text (abbreviated below as F). The adopted reading is given in italics, followed by the folio reading. Most of the corrections appeared first in the later folios of the seventeenth century or in eighteenth-century editions. In the case of a few readings adopted from modern editions, the editor's name is given in parentheses.

I, i, 36 *promises. Her dispositions* promises her dispositions 48 *have.* have— 54 *How ... that* (appears after l. 55 in F) 83 *above me.* above me 124 *got* goe 142 *ten,* two, 153 *wear* were

I, ii, 18 *Rossillion* Rosignoll

I, iii, 19 *and I will* and w will 82 *but or* but ore 108 *level;* *Dian no queen* leuell, Queene 164 *loneliness* louelinesse 170 *t' one to th' other* 'ton tooth to th'other 195 *intenible* intemible 242 *and* an

II, i, 3 *gain all,* gaine, all 42–43 *with his cicatrice, an emblem* his sicatrice, with an Embleme 62 *fee* see 109 *dear; I have* dear I have 144 *fits* shifts 155 *impostor* Impostrue 173 *nay* ne 192 *heaven* helpe

II, ii, 57 *An* And

II, iii, 75 s.d. (appears after l. 61 in F) 93 *her* here 124 *when* whence 129 *it is* is is 140 *indeed. What* indeed, what 286 *detested* detected

II, iv, 15 *fortunes* fortune

II, v, 26 *End* And 88 *Where ... Farewell* (assigned to Helena in F)

III, i, 23 *to th'* to'th the

III, ii, 9 *sold* hold 18 *E'en* In 64 *engrossest all* engrossest, all 108 *still-piecing* still-peering

III, iv, 7 *have* hane

III, v, 32 *le* la

III, vi, 32 *his* this   33 *ore* ours

III, vii, 19 *Resolved* Resolue

IV, i, 85 *art* are

IV, ii, 38 *may* (Sisson) make   *snare* (Sisson) scarre

IV, iii, 77–79 *They ... midnight* (assigned to Bertram in F)
85 *effected* affected   112 *Hush, hush* (assigned to Bertram in F)
131 *All's ... him* (assigned to Parolles in F)   184 *lordship* Lord
225 *our* your   248 *him!* (Alexander) him

IV, iv, 3 *'fore* for   16 *you,* your

IV, v, 18 *grass* grace   36 *name* maine

V, i, 6 s.d. *a Gentleman* a gentle Astringer

V, ii, 24 *similes* smiles   32 *under her* vnder

V, iii, 58–59 *carried, ... sender* carried ... sender,   71–72 *Which
... cesse* (assigned to the King in F)   122 *tax* taze   155 *sir,
sith* sir, sir   183 *them. Fairer* them fairer: 195 *it* hit   207 *sickens
but ... truth.* sickens: but ... truth,   216 *infinite cunning* insuite
comming   310 *are* is

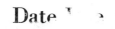